CULTURE SMART!
SERBIA

Lara Žmukić

·K·U·P·E·R·A·R·D·

ISBN 978 1 85733 659 7
This book is also available as an e-book: eISBN 978 1 85733 655 9

British Library Cataloguing in Publication Data
A CIP catalogue entry for this book is available from the British Library

First published in Great Britain
by Kuperard, an imprint of Bravo Ltd
59 Hutton Grove, London N12 8DS
Tel: +44 (0) 20 8446 2440   Fax: +44 (0) 20 8446 2441
www.culturesmart.co.uk
Inquiries: sales@kuperard.co.uk

Series Editor Geoffrey Chesler
Design Bobby Birchall

Printed in the USA

About the Author

LARA ŽMUKIĆ grew up in Montenegro and Serbia, trained as an economist, and graduated from the Novi Sad Faculty of Economics in northern Serbia. In 1997 she moved to Great Britain, where she met and married her husband. She worked in public-sector finance at a senior level for more than ten years before entering the private sector. Today she is the managing director of a media company specializing in the production and post-production of video content for a varied range of blue-chip clients, including the BBC, CNN, and Xerox. She divides her time between London, Belgrade, and Montenegro, where she still has many family connections, and she is a regular visitor to other countries in the Balkans.

The Culture Smart! series is continuing to expand.
For further information and latest titles visit
www.culturesmart.co.uk

The publishers would like to thank **CultureSmart!**Consulting for its help in researching and developing the concept for this series.

CultureSmart!Consulting creates tailor-made seminars and consultancy programs to meet a wide range of corporate, public-sector, and individual needs. Whether delivering courses on multicultural team building in the USA, preparing Chinese engineers for a posting in Europe, training call-center staff in India, or raising the awareness of police forces to the needs of diverse ethnic communities, it provides essential, practical, and powerful skills worldwide to an increasingly international workforce.

For details, visit www.culturesmartconsulting.com

CultureSmart!Consulting and **CultureSmart!** guides have both contributed to and featured regularly in the weekly travel program "Fast Track" on BBC World TV.

contents

contents

Map of Serbia

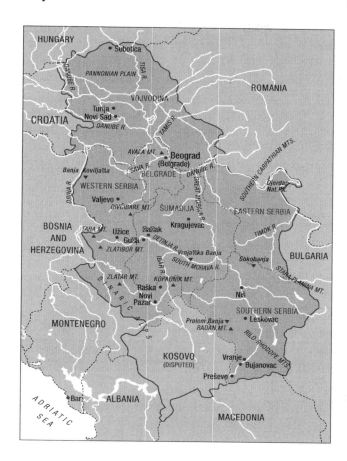

introduction

Filled with ancient sites and architectural riches, Serbia is a landlocked country positioned at the crossroads of central and southeastern Europe. A meeting place of different cultures and faiths, for centuries it was a major link between the Eastern and Western worlds, not only geographically but also politically and culturally. It is also a land of great beauty, with diverse climates and unusual landscapes.

Serbia was the dominant power in the former Yugoslavia, and during the protracted breakup of the Yugoslav republic it received a bad press in the West. However, the truth, as always, is much more nuanced and interesting than the accounts offered in the media. Some people may associate Serbia only with its recent conflicts and political turmoil; others will know about its world-famous music festivals, Exit and Guča, or its top-class athletes, such as the world's number one tennis player, Novak Djoković. Visitors will know it for its rich cuisine, the friendliness of its people, its stunning scenery, and its numerous monasteries, many in spectacular settings. It is a country steeped in history.

The Serbs are proud, passionate, and generous people with an independent streak. Since they first entered the region as warrior tribes allied with the Byzantine Empire, they have always had to fight for survival against powerful enemies, including the Ottoman Turks and the Habsburg Empire. Following the First World War, they took the lead in forming

independent Yugoslavia with the other Southern
Slavic peoples. They resisted Hitler heroically. Under
Tito's rule Yugoslavia steered an independent course,
separate from Western capitalism and Soviet
communism, until after his death in 1980 the
multinational state disintegrated amid bitter conflict.

The last of these conflicts, the war over the
secession of Kosovo, saw Serbia bombed by NATO
forces for two and a half months. This devastation,
combined with international isolation, caused the
Serbs to rise up against their leaders in the "Bulldozer
Revolution"—a campaign of civil resistance that
brought about democratic government in 2000. Today
Serbia has its gaze firmly set on Europe and the West.

Against this turbulent backdrop, the visitor to
Serbia needs to be well informed and sensitive to
people's feelings. *Culture Smart! Serbia* introduces you
to a diverse, complex, and dynamic society, and
provides an insight into Serbian values and the
Serbian way of life. It will tell you who the Serbs are,
what are they like, what they love, and what they
respect. It guides you through their customs, quirks,
and etiquette, and offers tips on communicating and
doing business with them. It will tell you how people
behave in particular situations and how they
experience their culture and customs, so that you
know how to respond appropriately. As a visitor to
Serbia, if you show interest and respect, you will
receive warm hospitality and lasting loyalty in return.

Key Facts

Official Name	Republic of Serbia, *Republika Srbija*	In the current administrative form since 2006
Capital City	Belgrade, *Beograd*	Population 1.1m in 2006
Other Major Cities	Novi Sad, Niš, Subotica, Valjevo, Kragujevac, Užice, Čačak	
Area	34,116 sq.mi (88,361 sq.km)	Landlocked country
Borders	Bosnia and Herzegovina, Croatia, Montenegro, Macedonia, Bulgaria, Romania, and Hungary	Used to border Albania through the disputed province of Kosovo
Climate	Cold winters with heavy precipitation; hot and humid summers	Conditions can vary across the country owing to the differences in terrain, and proximity to the plains or mountains.
Currency	Serbian dinar (RSD)	
Population	7,276,604 in 2011 (excl. Kosovo)	
Ethnic Makeup	Serbs 83%, Hungarians 4%, others 13%	
Language	Serbian. Cyrillic and Latin scripts used, with Cyrillic being the official one	
Religion	Serbian Orthodox 85%, Catholic 5.5%, Muslim 3.2%, Protestant 1.1%, unspecified 2.6%, other, unknown, or atheist 2.6% (2002 census)	

Government	Parliamentary republic. The president is head of state; the prime minister is head of the government. President elected by direct vote for a five-year term. The National Assembly has 250 seats, elected by party lists.	Two administrative divisions, Vojvodina and Serbia proper, and 167 municipalities; the disputed province of Kosovo was another administrative division.
Media	Public TV network: Radio Television of Serbia: RTS1 and RTS2. Private networks: Pink, B92, Prva, and Happy TV. Satellite and cable TV available. Some English channels	Public radio broadcaster: RTS, with channels RB1, RB2, RB4, and 202. Private stations: B92, Radio Index, Focus, Radio S
Press	Main daily broadsheets: *Politika* and *Danas*. Daily tabloids: *Večernje Novosti*, *Blic*, *Pravda*, *Press*, and *Kurir*. Weekly newspapers and periodicals: *Vreme*, *Nedeljni Telegraf*, and *Nin*. Some foreign-language publications available at bookshops and kiosks in major cities.	
Electricity	220 volts, 50 HZ	Standard European two-prong plug; UK and US devices require an adapter
Video/TV	PAL. DVB-T is being introduced.	Analogue PAL to be abandoned by 2015.
Internet Domain	.rs .srb	
Telephone	Serbia's country code is 381. Belgrade city: 11	Domestic access code 0. To dial abroad, dial 00.
Time Zone	Central European Time: GMT +1	

chapter one

LAND & PEOPLE

GEOGRAPHY

Serbia lies at the crossroads of central and southern
Europe, nestled in the Balkan region between the four
other republics that comprised the former Yugoslavia—
Bosnia and Herzegovina, Croatia, Montenegro, and
Macedonia—and Albania, with the disputed province
of Kosovo to the south and Bulgaria, Romania, and
Hungary to the east and north.

The country is landlocked, reliant principally on
the Montenegrin port of Bar for access to the sea.
Its landmass covers a total of 29,913 sq. miles
(77,474 sq. km) with a total border length of more
than 1,259 miles (2,026 km) excluding the disputed
province of Kosovo.

The northern third of Serbia is located entirely in
the Pannonian Plain, a fertile lowland basin
surrounded by mountains, which also encompasses
parts of Hungary, Croatia, Romania, Slovakia, Slovenia,
Austria, and Ukraine. The Serbian part belongs to the
autonomous province of Vojvodina, with the capital,
Belgrade, lying on the southernmost boundary.

In the north, Europe's second longest river, the
Danube, flows through the picturesque Vojvodina
flatlands and the national parks of Fruška Gora and
Đerdap, meeting the Sava River at Belgrade. The

Danube is important to pan-European trade, being part of a route stretching from Rotterdam on the North Sea to Sulina on the Black Sea, giving Serbia shipping access to these ports. During the 1999 NATO bombing, this artery was disrupted by the destruction of three Serbian bridges; the debris was not cleared until 2002.

Most Serbian rivers drain to the Black Sea by way of the Danube. Along its 368-mile (588-km) course through Serbia (approximately 10 percent of its overall length), the main tributaries are the rivers Tisa, Sava, Tamiš, Morava, Drina, Ibar, and Timok. Together these rivers provide a drainage basin covering the entire Serbian territory.

The rivers caused the flooding that turned Vojvodina into marshy swampland by the end of the sixteenth century. To counter this, as well as for irrigation, navigation, tourism, fishing, and hunting, an elaborate system of canals began to be built in the eighteenth century.

The Danube–Tisa–Danube canal system is the largest in Serbia, and extends the Danube and the Tisa rivers in the Bačka and Banat districts of Vojvodina, dominating the region. The canal is 577 miles (929 km) in length, of which 400 miles (664 km) are navigable. Approximately 4 million metric tons of goods, mainly gravel, metals, and ores, are transported on this waterway annually.

The greater part of the rest of Serbia is mountainous. The geology is varied, consisting of limestone basins, rolling hills, and formations of significant mineral deposits. These include lignite, iron, copper, lead, and zinc—indeed, mining was a cornerstone of the regional economy during the Communist period, albeit paralyzed during the subsequent conflicts.

Central Serbia has forested hills and low-to-medium mountains, alternating with picturesque rivers and creeks. Southeast of Belgrade, the Great Morava and South Morava Rivers form the main

communication route south toward Niš and Skopje in Macedonia.

Four mountain ranges extend into Serbian territory: the Rilo–Rhodope range stretches along the South Morava River. In the southeast, the Rhodope Mountains meet the Balkan Mountains. Following the course of the Morava River, the Balkan Mountains meet the Southern Carpathian range, which stretches across eastern Serbia and runs through central Europe. Finally, the Dinaric Alps cover western and central Serbia, following the Drina River and the border with Bosnia and Herzegovina.

The region is prone to seismic activity: major earthquakes in the twentieth century ranged between 5.0 and 6.0 on the Richter scale. Transform fault lines in the region can cause shallow, moderate quakes, which luckily have never been devastating. In 2010 there was a 5.4-magnitude earthquake, its epicenter 78 miles (125 km) south of Belgrade.

Midžor peak in the Balkan Mountains is the highest point in eastern Serbia, at 7,113 feet (2,168 m). Further south in disputed Kosovo, the Djeravica peak on Prokletije on the Bulgarian border is the highest point of the Dinaric Alps, at 8,714 feet (2,656 m). There are more than thirty mountains in Serbia higher than 5,000 feet (1,500 m).

The best-known mountain in Serbia is Kopaonik, a world-class tourist ski resort, just over 155 miles (250 km, six hours' journey) from Belgrade. Its highest peak is Pančić (6,617 ft / 2,017 m), and its national park covers 46 square miles (118 sq. km). Other noted mountains with major resorts are Stara Planina, Zlatibor, Tara, and Divčibare.

CLIMATE

Mountain ranges of different elevations, large river basins, and proximity to the Adriatic Sea all contribute to Serbia's diverse climate. In the north, along the flatlands of Vojvodina, a continental climate dominates, with hot, humid summers and freezing winters, and ample rainfall for agricultural development. An Adriatic or Mediterranean climate prevails in the south, with hot, dry summers, and cold winters with heavy inland snowfall. The mountains of Serbia naturally experience heavy winter snowfall: January is the coldest month and the ski season generally runs from December to March, although it often snows from early November.

Average temperatures in Serbia range from 14° to 32°F (–10° to 0°C) in winter, and from 59° to 86°F (15° to 30°C) in summer. Although August is the hottest month, autumn is often warmer than spring, making it the most moderate time of year to visit. Peak summer (July/August) is often unbearably hot in Belgrade and Vojvodina, and residents flock to nearby coasts to avoid the stifling heat.

Because of the mountainous territory, various winds also contribute to climate differences in Serbia. The most famous of the Serbian winds is the Košava, a cold, southeastern wind that blows destructively for several days, leaving dry, sunny weather in the summer and freezing subzero temperatures in the winter. Starting in the Carpathian Mountains, the wind spreads from Hungary in the north to Niš in the south via Belgrade. Although there is much talk of harnessing this wind power for renewable energy purposes (along with hydroelectricity, biomass, and solar power), the renewable energy sector is still embryonic.

When traveling in winter, medium-weight clothing with a heavy overcoat and heavy snow boots are necessary. In summer, lightweight clothing is fine, including a light raincoat and sandals or light shoes. In spring and fall there can be considerable variations in temperature in a single day, so it is best to go prepared for both light winter and summer weather if you are traveling at these times.

THE PEOPLE

The population of Serbia is around 7.3 million (2011 estimate), not including the Kosovan population of about 2.1 million. Most people live in urban areas, 1.7 million of these in Belgrade.

Serbia has an aging population and one of the lowest birthrates in Europe. The population has declined over the last twenty years, leading to the degeneration of rural areas and looming political and economic problems regarding pensions. Currently, there are only 1.6 economically active people per pensioner, leaving a massive shortfall in the national pension pot, a problem compounded by a bloated state bureaucracy.

However, in Serbia people do not live as long as their European neighbors; life expectancy is only seventy-one for men and seventy-seven for women.

As a result of its central location in the region, Serbia is home to an assortment of minorities: there are approximately thirty-seven different nationalities. However, net migration is currently minimal, and the wars of the 1990s left the population more Serbian. According to the 2002 census, 83 percent of the population is Serb, 3.9 percent Hungarian, 1.4 percent Romany (Gypsy), 1.8 percent Bosniak, 0.9 percent Montenegrin, and 9.1 percent other.

The official language is Serbian, and 88 percent of the population speak it as a first language. It is virtually identical to the other languages in the region— Croatian, Bosnian, or Montenegrin, for example—by virtue of being simply a regional variation of what was previously the common language of Yugoslavia, formerly labeled "Serbo-Croatian" and now sometimes described internationally as BCS (Bosnian / Croatian / Serbian). Locals often refer to their own dialect as "the local language," meaning that it is also understood in all the former Yugoslav republics. One key difference is that Serbs use the Cyrillic script for their written language, in contrast to the other countries, which use the Latin script.

At school, ethnic minorities often learn their mother tongue as their first language and Serbian only second. Hungarian is the second most widely spoken language in Serbia, with almost 4 percent of people calling it their mother tongue. In Vojvodina, home to the majority of ethnic migrants, Serbian, Hungarian, Romanian, Slovak, Croatian, and Rusyn (also known as Ruthenian) are all official languages.

The dissolution of the former Yugoslavia and the wars of the 1990s have left Serbia with long-lasting refugee problems. Following the wars in Croatia and Bosnia and Herzegovina (1991–6), more than 200,000 refugees crossed into Serbia and have been formally integrated and granted citizenship. They were mostly people of Serbian heritage, those with the connections and resources to make it back to the motherland. Approximately two-thirds of them returned from Croatia and a third from Bosnia and Herzegovina.

After the 1999 NATO intervention in favor of the Kosovo Albanians, 300,000 people, again those of Serbian heritage and other non-Albanian peoples, fled Kosovo for Serbia. The majority are still of indeterminate status. According to the UN Refugee Agency (UNHCR), Serbia currently has one of the largest displaced populations in Europe. More than 300,000 people of concern are living in Serbia (refugees, asylum seekers, returnees, stateless people, and others); the majority are Kosovars with the status of internally displaced persons.

REGIONS AND CITIES

Serbia has six geographically distinct regions: Vojvodina, Belgrade, Western Serbia, Eastern Serbia, Šumadija, and Southern Serbia.

Vojvodina is the northernmost province, spreading from just north of Belgrade to the borders with Hungary and Romania. Dotted with fields, orchards, and vineyards, the area contains the fertile Pannonian Plain, numerous waterways, and the Fruška Gora, the only mountain on the plain, lying just south of the course of the Danube. It is the agricultural heart of Serbia, with a population of 2 million, or 27 percent of the total.

The region is demographically diverse, and its people are known for their calm and friendly nature, their spicy cuisine, and their folk music, characterized by string orchestras and the *tamburitza*, a sort of long-necked lute.

As well as the monotonous flatlands of the plain, there are two sandy regions in Vojvodina: the Subotica sands near the border with Hungary, and the larger Deliblato sands. Deliblato is the largest sandy terrain in Europe, and it was once part of a vast prehistoric desert—the "European Sahara"—that emerged with the retreat of the Pannonian Sea. The sand is now anchored with vegetation and has been restored by humans in a planned fashion, but this is nevertheless an area of exceptional beauty and scientific interest, with rich biodiversity and unique undulating dunes.

Novi Sad is the political and cultural capital of Vojvodina and Serbia's second city. Subotica,

Zrenjanin, Pančevo, and Sremska Mitrovica are other noted cities in the region. Novi Sad is well-known for its Austro-Hungarian heritage. The old town is often referred to as the "Serbian Athens," with architectural styles including Gothic, Baroque, Art Nouveau, and Neoclassic. These buildings now house official institutions, museums, and galleries, and help make Novi Sad one of the historical treasures of Europe.

Belgrade with its surrounding region is the most developed part of the country. It is located at the confluence of the Danube and Sava Rivers, at the southern edge of the Pannonian Plain. It is home to 1.7 million people (15 percent of the country's population) and is responsible for 40 percent of

Serbia's GDP. The area has been continuously populated since Neolithic times, and its strategic location has seen it fought over in more than a hundred wars.

Western Serbia rises from fertile plains and lower mountains to the high peaks of the Dinaric Alps, in particular the mountains of Tara, Zlatibor, and Zlatar. These are Serbia's highest mountains, with dense coniferous forests and rich wildlife—a great place for nature lovers.

"Ethno-villages" (see pages 68 and 125) are scattered around this region, attracting tourists to settlements constructed in the traditional style from wood, with an open fire inside, and often without electricity. The mountainous terrain means there are few major cities in western Serbia. The most prominent are Užice and Valjevo, industrial towns on the Detinja River that suffered disproportionately during NATO's bombing of the region.

Eastern Serbia is even more sparsely populated and wild. The area is famous for its clean air and medicinal plants, with orchards and vineyards covering the banks of the Danube as it stretches east toward the Black Sea. Gorges, canyons, and caves form the spectacular terrain of the region, the eastern sections of the Carpathian and Balkan Mountains.

The remoteness of eastern Serbia and the unusual geological formations of the Carpathians contribute to a persisting pagan belief system in the area and a general reverence for nature. There is barely a village in eastern Serbia without a local "wise man" (or woman) who can "see" into the supernatural realm.

Šumadija (meaning "forest land") is the central part of Serbia, named after the density of its forests. The Morava and Ibar River valleys dominate this part of the country, along with numerous medium-sized mountains. The first of these, Mount Avala, is located just south of Belgrade, like a gateway to the city. Lunch on the mount is a matter of prestige among Belgradians, and it is the best place from which to view the whole city.

The villages of central Serbia are rich and fertile, with agricultural production on a smaller and more localized scale than in Vojvodina and with a greater emphasis on fruit than grain crops. In autumn, each village is transformed into an informal factory processing and preserving the produce from the summer harvest into jams, juices, and conserves. The forests are also a rich source of wild foodstuffs, in particular Serbian truffles and mushrooms, which often find their way into the international markets.

The biggest city in this region is Kragujevac, the fourth largest in Serbia. A trading center for centuries, Kragujevac is best known for its automotive and arms manufacturing industries. The formerly state-owned Zastava Automobiles was established here in 1953; it produced the famous "Yugo," sometimes called "the worst car ever," but more objectively a simple, cheap Communist-era vehicle that can still be seen on the roads of eastern Europe. After the industrial depression of the 1990s, Zastava was sold to Fiat in 2008. There are currently high hopes that renewed automobile manufacturing in the region will boost the economy and earn much-needed foreign currency.

Southern Serbia encompasses the area from the city of Niš down to the border with Macedonia, and is one of the least developed regions in the country because of its proximity to Kosovo and the wars that have plagued the area, culminating in Kosovo's declaration of independence in 2008.

Around one million people live in southern Serbia, approximately 96 percent Serb and the remainder Albanian. Along the border with Kosovo, the Albanian influence is greatest and power is shared between ethnic Serb and Albanian parties, with education provided in both the Albanian and Serbian languages.

Southern Serbia is mountainous, but some of the highest peaks of the Dinaric range to the south now belong to the Republic of Kosovo rather than to Serbia. On the eastern side, the start of the Rhodope mountain range extends toward Bulgaria and Greece.

The area is dominated by a number of river valleys. The South Morava valley extends south from Serbia to Macedonia, whereas the Nišava valley forms an ancient communication route into Bulgaria and contains the stunning nature reserve of the Sićevo Gorge.

Niš is the major city in this part of Serbia, and the third largest overall. Two major communication lines intersect at Niš—the road connecting Asia Minor to Europe, and the road connecting the Black Sea to the Mediterranean. Niš has been a major center since ancient times, notable for producing three Roman emperors, including the first Christian emperor, Constantine the Great. Fittingly, Niš is home to Serbia's oldest Christian church, dedicated to the apostles Peter and Paul and founded in the fourth century. Today Niš is an important industrial center, producing tobacco, machinery, and textiles, among other things.

A BRIEF HISTORY
Early History and the Middle Ages

There is evidence of Neolithic cultures in the Balkan region dating back to 6500 BCE. From around 1000 BCE, Classical peoples such as the Illyrians, Dacians, and Thracians began to inhabit the region. Rome started conquering the Balkans in the second century CE, and the area of modern Serbia encompasses, wholly or in part, the Roman provinces of Moesia, Pannonia, Praevalitana, Dalmatia, Dacia, and Macedonia. Subsequently, with the division of

the Roman Empire in 395, these lands became part of the Eastern Roman Empire, later called the Byzantine Empire. In the third to seventh centuries Slav migration started to alter the demography of the region fundamentally.

An official Byzantine history, *The Administration of the Empire*, written by Emperor Constantine VII (r. 913–59), mentions the "Unknown Archont" who led the Slavic Serbian population from their mythical homeland Bojka, or White Serbia, in the north, to settle in the Balkan region as military allies of the empire around 610 CE.

When the Muslim Avar Khanate threatened the Byzantine hold on the Balkan Peninsula, the Byzantine emperor Heraclius granted the Serbs land near the modern city of Thessaloniki in Greece to serve as a last defense. However, the Unknown Archont was unhappy with the deal and led his people back across the Sava River, to return only when a more suitable award was offered—the territory that forms present-day Bosnia and Herzegovina, Montenegro, and eastern Serbia.

At that time, the Serb settlements were still independent of the Western/Roman and Eastern/Greek Empires. The Serb population was organized in several provinces between the Morava River to the east and the Stolin River to the west, and a political concordat between the Frankish and Byzantine Empires recognized them as a sociopolitical entity without a hereditary leadership.

The Serbs developed a Byzantine-Slavic culture, and during the ninth century, the ruling class of one of the first Serbian principalities, Raška, accepted

Christianity in exchange for international recognition and the right to hereditary titles. The first recognized kingdom, called Duklja (in Latin Doclea, later Zeta), emerged in the twelfth century. Of the Serbian nobility, the Nemanjić family dominated: the founder of the Serbian state (and later empire), Stefan Nemanja (1113–99), was Grand Prince of Raška from 1166 to 1196.

The rise of Raška and the house of Nemanjić oversaw territorial expansion at the expense of the Bulgarian and Byzantine Empires. Rastko, the youngest son of Stefan Nemanja and a monk by education, traveled throughout the Byzantine lands, returning convinced that establishing a permanent tie was crucial to the advancement of his house's interests. In 1219, Constantinople recognized him as the first archbishop of the Serbs and the founder of the Serbian Orthodox Church. This agreement saw the Serbs gain full religious and political independence, and Rastko, known by his monastic name of Sava, became one of the most important figures in Serbian history.

The Serbian Empire

In the fourteenth century, King Stefan Uroš IV Dušan proclaimed the Serbian Empire, naming himself first Tsar and "Emperor of the Serbs and Greeks." Serbia had extended its borders to include access to three seas—the Adriatic, the Black Sea, and

the Aegean—and had doubled its former territory.
With such expansion came the opening up of new
trade routes, so the economy grew and the country
flourished. This made Serbia one of the most
developed countries in Europe at the time.

Together with Pope Innocent VI, Dušan planned
a crusade against the threatening
Turks, only to die in mysterious
circumstances while on campaign
in 1355. His older son Uroš, known
by the epithet "the Weak,"
succeeded him. The Serb nobility
supported Uroš by recognizing him
as emperor, but they ignored his
instructions. He was able neither to
repel foreign attack nor to conquer
lands anew, and his lack of
authority and power led to the
gradual decline of his father's great empire.

In the decades that followed Dušan's death, the
Serbian Empire consisted of several warring
kingdoms and principalities vying for dominance or
independence. The Kingdom of Bosnia and the
expanding Duchy of Herzegovina began to
dominate, extending influence and territory.
Nevertheless, Ottoman Turkish forces arriving in the
Balkans encountered a patchwork of principalities
that failed to unite to fight for their own survival.

The Ottoman Period
The Battle of Maritsa (1371) took place at the Maritsa
River in present-day Greece and sowed the seeds of
future Ottoman success. The Serbs, overconfident,

arrived in greater numbers and were convinced of imminent victory; however, they let their guard down and were stormed in the middle of the night (drunk, as the myth claims). Almost all the leading Serb nobles were dead by morning, leaving the army fractured and the competing heirs divided.

The fabled Battle of Kosovo (1389) was an attempt by the ruling families of Serbia to unite under Prince Lazar Hrebeljanović and save their estates from Sultan Murad I's advancing army. The battle was a bloodbath, both armies being wiped out and both commanders dying in battle.

When Ottoman reinforcements eventually moved in from the east over the following years, they found the Serbs unable to raise an adequate army. One by one the Serb rulers became unwilling vassals of the Turks without putting up a fight. The Serbian nobility swore an oath of allegiance to the Sultan and sent Christian men to fight in the Muslim Ottoman army.

The Ottoman administrative system, although a meritocracy, reserved the highest positions for Muslims. Nevertheless, the new balance of power in the Balkans afforded Serbs the possibility of advancement. A familiar name from this period was Mehmed Paša Sokolović, one of a dozen Serbs who directly served the Sultan as Grand Vizier, effectively running the empire. Sokolović is renowned for serving under no fewer than three Sultans.

During the fifteenth and sixteenth centuries, the Ottoman

Empire extended its borders from Europe to North Africa. Suleiman the Magnificent (1520–66) captured Belgrade in 1521, and also conquered the southern and central parts of the Kingdom of Hungary. Finally, the unsuccessful siege of Vienna in 1532 led to his retreat. Although Ottoman rule over much of southeastern Europe was still maintained, this defeat saw the end of Ottoman expansion and the slow but unremitting advance of the Habsburgs.

The Austrian Period

Habsburg invasions and rebellions continually challenged Ottoman rule, concluding with the Austro-Ottoman Wars at the end of the seventeenth century, mostly centered on Hungary. The Peace Treaty of Karlovci, signed on January 26, 1699, in Sremski Karlovci (in modern Serbia), spelled the end of Ottoman rule in much of the region.

The treaty ceded Vojvodina to the Habsburg Empire, but also returned much of Serbian territory to the Ottomans, causing a massive Serb migration. Serbs left Kosovo and central Serbia, seeking refuge across the Danube under the Austrian crown. The declining Ottoman Empire grew increasingly brutal in its remaining territories and in the Belgrade Pašaluk (province), intensifying its persecution of the Christian population. Between 1688 and 1791 the Habsburgs captured Belgrade three times; each time it was recaptured and razed to the ground by the Ottomans.

Although the Serb population failed to accept either of the ruling dynasties truly as their own sovereigns, Christian Habsburg rule was naturally more tolerable. Over the next two centuries, the Serbs acquired status as protectors of the realm by manning the frontier of the Habsburg Empire. This status, in addition to privileges such as tax exemptions and increasing autonomy within the empire, set the Serbs on a course by which each successive fight against the Ottomans would meet with greater success.

However, the Serbs' long-perceived ally would become their chief enemy in the twentieth century, and the greatest threat to a nascent Serbian state

The Serbian Revolution

Successive national uprisings against their Ottoman masters between 1804 and 1817 culminated in the recognition of Serb autonomy under Ottoman suzerainty. The Serbian constitution adopted in 1835 abolished feudalism and serfdom, and established the state as a modern constitutional monarchy. In 1878 the Congress of Berlin

formally recognized the independence of the Principality of Serbia, and in 1882 the expanded principality became a kingdom.

The Balkan Wars and the Great War

A series of treaties concluding in 1912 saw the Balkan League, an alliance of Serbia, Montenegro,

Greece, and Bulgaria, gaining independence from
the Ottoman Empire. However, ethnic populations in
the areas still under Ottoman control were seeking
sovereignty, and in order to liberate them the league
attacked the Ottoman Empire in October 1912. Two
conflicts, known as the Balkan Wars, took place
between 1912 and 1913, during which the Ottoman
Empire lost virtually all its remaining possessions in
the region.

During these two years alone, the Kingdom of
Serbia expanded its territory into Kosovo,
Macedonia, and Raška. The territory of Serbia
became 80 percent greater than before the war, and
its population grew by 50 percent. Russia, wary of
Austro-Hungarian expansionism to its west,
supported Serbia and the league as a bulwark against
its enemy.

The great power politics that dominated Europe
at this time had no place for nascent nation-states.
Surprising alliances were forged as each power vied
for influence in the changing political landscape. For

example, past enemies such as Great Britain and France developed close ties in order to check the development of the German Empire. Germany's industrial ambitions required access to resources and oil from the Middle East, and so the Austro-Hungarian Empire, feeling encircled and isolated, provided a measure of support. In return, Germany gave carte blanche to the expansionist pretensions of Habsburg foreign policy, which was then focused on the eradication of the Kingdom of Serbia. The Habsburg Empire viewed the increasing ties between Serbia and Russia as a threat to their influence, and was concerned about the growing strength of the Serbian nation and its territorial ambitions.

It was in this climate that Gavrilo Princip, a Serb nationalist, assassinated the heir to the Austro-Hungarian throne, Archduke Franz Ferdinand, in Sarajevo on June 28, 1914, an event that was to trigger the First World War.

Initially, Serbia was successful in the first major battles of the war against Austria-Hungary. However, the greater forces of the German, Austro-Hungarian, and Bulgarian alliance forced the Serbs to flee south into exile in Greece. There they reformed their battalions before returning to the Macedonian (Salonika) front. Serbia received substantial help from the French and the British, and in September 1918 the army helped force the capitulation of Bulgaria and the

Austro-Hungarian Empire. This victory came at a great price for Serbia, however, with the total number of casualties estimated at one million, more than a quarter of the country's prewar population and more than half the overall male population.

For around a century until this point, Serbian politicians, irrespective of their political persuasion, had been dedicated to the concept of a unified Serbian nation. This concept had been set out in 1844 by Ilija Garašanin, an exiled Serbian statesman who took ideas from the German and French models of nationhood, balancing the interests of the current Serbian state with its complex demographics and history.

The Kingdom of Yugoslavia

On December 1, 1918, Garašanin's idea finally became a reality and the Kingdom of Serbs, Croats,

and Slovenes was created. While many intellectuals favored the unification of the Southern Slavs into one state, the Serbian high command and many leading statesmen, still roused by their victory in the war, vehemently opposed this and preferred a smaller, demographically exclusive Serbia. Nevertheless, the recognition of this new state at the Treaty of Versailles ushered in a new era for Serbia: it satisfied the centuries-old dream of an independent and free Serbian nation.

From the start, the kingdom had an uphill battle to consolidate its position. Already decimated by the First World War, with a predominantly rural population and very few commercial farmers, the new state found it difficult to organize labor, build the economy, and satisfy the expectations of its populace. The kingdom did not have the technical know-how or capital to build an industrial or manufacturing base, and so developed an agroexport-based economy by borrowing money from the West during the 1920s. However, when these debts were called in as the Great Depression began, the kingdom was forced to default and suffered doubly as hastily erected trade barriers destroyed the agricultural export market. Under these difficult conditions, from 1933 onward, the kingdom allowed itself to become economically dependent on Nazi Germany.

Internally, Serb politicians began to regard Serbia as the cornerstone of the Yugoslav union, and pushed Serbocentric policies that riled the Croatian factions. This conflict came to a head in 1929, when a member of the Serb majority, Puniša Račić, shot five members of the Croatian Peasant Party in the Constituent Assembly, killing two immediately and fatally wounding the leader of the party.  The opposition immediately withdrew from parliament and King Aleksandar Karadjordjević abolished parliament, tore up the constitution, and proclaimed the Kingdom of Yugoslavia ("Southern Slavs") on January 6, 1929. This was effectively a personal dictatorship with all executive power deriving from the king.

The Second World War

By 1940, all the countries adjoining Yugoslavia, except Greece, had signed treaties with Hitler's Germany. Although Yugoslavia was under pressure to join the Axis powers, massive public demonstrations erupted across the country against any such alliance. A coup d'état brought in a replacement government that subsequently withdrew all Yugoslav support for the Axis. This was a risky move because, although the Yugoslav rulers opposed the Nazis, they knew that should Germany attack, no neighboring country would help.

Hitler saw the coup as an insult and was determined to exact revenge. In April 1941, Germany heavily bombed Belgrade and other major cities. German ground forces invaded from neighboring countries, forcing the Royal Yugoslav Government and King Peter II to flee to exile in London.

The Kingdom of Yugoslavia was dissolved and divided up into separate administrative regions, each becoming a Nazi puppet state. Serbia fell under the German military administration led by Serbian General Milan Nedić, while Croatia and Bosnia and Herzegovina were ruled by the fascist Croatian nationalist army, Ustaše, as the Independent State of Croatia (NDH), the rest of the country being divided up among the other Axis powers, including Italy in the south, Hungary in the northwest, and Bulgaria in the southeast.

During this time, Serbia descended into internal conflict between royalist Četniks led by Draža Mihailović, Communist Partisans led by Josip Broz Tito, and General Nedić's pro-German units. Nazi racial laws came into force, and concentration camps were established around the country, killing around 40,000 Serbian Jews, Roma, and other political prisoners and resistance fighters.

The Independent State of Croatia persecuted Serbs as well as Jews and Roma, with the concentration camp of Jasenovac being responsible for 500,000 to 700,000 deaths, mostly believed to be of Serbs killed by the Ustaše. Unsurprisingly, animosity between Serbs and Croats continues to this day.

Many across Yugoslavia opposed the occupation and their rulers' genocidal policies, and joined the Partisans, the national liberation army created by the Communist Party and headed by Josip Broz Tito. This pan-Yugoslav force united Serbs, Croats, Slovenes, Jews, and Muslims in a revolutionary war against the Nazis. Whereas Četnik royalists had backed down in the face of Nazi reprisal massacres against civilians, the Partisans refused to compromise.

By the end of 1944 Serbia was liberated, and the remaining parts of Yugoslavia were freed a few months later. Again, Yugoslavia had suffered great losses during the war, losing about a million people to the conflict.

Yugoslavia under Tito

After the bloodbath of the Second World War, the only unifying force with any power in Yugoslavia was the Partisans, together with the Communist Party. The League of Communists of Yugoslavia abolished the monarchy, undermined the authority of the Church, and in 1945 established a single-party state

of which Tito became the first president. This new Socialist Federal Republic of Yugoslavia (SFRY) consisted of six constituent republics, one

of which was the Socialist Republic of Serbia.

The Communist movement suppressed any sign of dissent or nationalist politics, seeing separatism as the biggest threat to the new republic. After the expected Stalinist-inspired show trials, Tito suddenly turned his back on the USSR in 1948, wary of domination by the Soviet Union. Many believe the Korean conflict distracted the Soviet leadership and military from invading Yugoslavia at this point, as this rift made enemies out of former comrades.

In 1949 two islands in the Adriatic Sea, Goli Otok and nearby St. Grgur (in present-day Croatia), were officially turned into high-security prisons and labor camps. These secret institutions ran for seven years, receiving political prisoners from all over Yugoslavia.

Most were alleged Stalinists, sympathetic toward the Soviet Union, but there were also other political dissidents, and even some who put the Church before the Party.

Although Tito is often characterized in the West as a dictator and authoritarian, in his time he was a symbol of unity for Yugoslavs, and many have fond memories of his rule. He was extremely popular both within Yugoslavia and abroad. Tito created his own special brand of socialism, with "Brotherhood and Unity" as its motto; a self-managed workforce, state-owned property, and a small hint of a market economy. Initially Tito copied the Soviet model, but soon turned toward the West for a more hybrid approach. With financial loans from both East and West, he implemented reforms that created an economy open to private enterprise, and a culture with relaxed restrictions on freedom of speech and religious expression. Many Serbs today remember Tito's times with nostalgia as happy times when the quality of life was good, jobs were secure and well paying, neighbors baked each other cakes, and they had a leader they trusted.

President Tito died in May 1980, having become increasingly ill over the previous year. A charismatic and popular leader, he was given the largest state funeral in history, attended by delegates from 128 countries.

The Fall of Yugoslavia, and Serbia Today
Tito's death saw a rise in nationalism and ethnic tensions in the six Yugoslav republics, as each began to pursue its own interests. Serbia, the largest and

most populous of the republics, strove for political dominion over the Federation, and favored the existing state-planned economy. Slovenia and Croatia favored Western-style market reforms, and indeed Croatia was keen to seek political autonomy, which in turn led its domestic Serb communities to push for their own independence.

Rising inflation and economic stagnation became another cause of tension between the republics. After the boom years of the 1960s, the 1970s had seen living standards fall as Western economies entered recession and blocked Yugoslav exports, creating another debt problem. Yugoslavia turned to the IMF for further loans, which were dependent on macroeconomic reforms that chipped away at the state industrial sector and the welfare state.

Prime Minister Ante Markovic implemented further economic changes at the end of the 1980s that included partial privatizations, trade liberalization, and other market-oriented reforms. Although they offered a temporary respite from runaway inflation, these structural changes led to greater problems in the industrial sector and state-owned enterprises, and GDP continued to decline. To his political opponents Markovic was seen as being in league with the USA and hostile to socialism—a traitor to Yugoslavia.

By the 1990s Yugoslavia's economy was effectively controlled by the IMF. Rather than funding social or economic programs, the Yugoslav central bank was compelled to funnel state revenue back to private creditors in London and Paris, to service the debt. The republics were left to fend for themselves, and secessionist feelings intensified. Each republic attempted to increase its own economic autonomy, for example by refusing to pay federal taxes or enforce federal customs dues. The previously well-developed heavy industry sector all but disappeared, socially owned enterprises could not pay their workers, the welfare state vanished, wages fell, unemployment rocketed, and the whole Communist-era concept of a socially owned, worker-managed economy was destroyed.

In 1989 Slobodan Milošević came to power as president of Serbia, largely on a Serb-nationalist ticket that saw him supporting Serbs in Kosovo who were claiming oppression by the ethnic Albanian majority. His opponents accused him of attempting to reintroduce Serb hegemony over the region, and of fostering nationalism, which had been anathema in Communist-era "Brotherhood and Unity" Yugoslavia. Milošević started to consolidate his power by tightening control over the governments of Vojvodina and Kosovo provinces, effectively taking veto control over the eight-member Yugoslav Presidency Council, where four votes could now be guaranteed as a minimum—Serbia, Montenegro, Vojvodina, and Kosovo.

This naturally caused aggravation within the governments of the other republics. In this climate the League of Communists of Yugoslavia was convened in 1990 to try to reform the Federation. Slovenia and Croatia pushed for greater devolved power; Serbia for "one person one vote," which would have given the Serbs a clear majority in any federal decision making. In the ensuing impasse the league dissolved, officially ending the one-party system and establishing a multiparty system within each individual republic. Democratization saw reformist parties elected peacefully in Croatia and Slovenia and Communist rule confirmed in Serbia.

Even within Serbia's nominal multiparty democracy, Milošević maintained power by controlling the media and suppressing dissent. Authoritarian laws were enacted to protect federal institutions and symbols and to restrict freedom of speech. These allowed blackouts of independent media coverage, for example that of antigovernment protests. Anyone who ridiculed the government was liable for arrest, so political opponents were systematically criminalized. Under these conditions a tense climate of ultranationalism was established.

In Croatia, the leading nationalist party promised to "defend Croatia from Milošević," officially reducing the status of Serbs living there from "constituent nationals" to a "national minority" and thus downgrading them to the status of other minorities. This caused great alarm among Croatian Serbs, many of whom could still remember Jasenovac and persecution by the Ustaše during the Second World War.

The Wars of Secession
In 1991, Slovenia and Croatia declared independence from Yugoslavia, triggering a series of wars. The Yugoslav People's Army (JNA) attempted to prevent the secession of Slovenia during the Ten-Day War, which was halted when the breakaway republics agreed to delay their push for autonomy. But soon

after, Croatia announced its own secession and the Croatian War of Independence started, initially with Croatian Serb rebels fighting Croatian national paramilitary units. The rebels were soon aided by the JNA, in a conflict that was to affect the whole country.

After a ceasefire in 1992, the international community recognized the Republic of Croatia as a sovereign state. The United Nations Protection Force (UNPROFOR) was deployed to keep the peace; fighting was to continue sporadically for another three years. The JNA was formally dissolved and Croatia ended the war with total victory, having won independence and preserved her borders.

By contrast, Macedonia's declaration of independence in 1991 was a peaceful affair with no fighting. This was not the case with Bosnia and Herzegovina, which declared its independence in 1992, thus triggering the Bosnian War and the infamous siege of Sarajevo. This conflict eventually resulted in 100,000 dead by 1995, in the most devastating fighting in Europe since the Second World War.

Bosnia and Herzegovina was the most ethnically mixed of the republics, with mutual hostility between Bosnian Serbs, Bosnian Croats, and Bosnian Muslims (Bosniaks). Hence the protracted and bloody nature of the war. Bosnia's Serb faction was led by the ultranationalist Radovan Karadzić, who attempted to link the disjointed Serb-populated territories. Although initially dominant, Serb forces started to lose ground after the Bosniak–Croat alliance in 1994 and then the NATO bombing campaign against them in 1995.

As before, Serbs in Bosnia were strongly against the separation of Bosnia and Herzegovina from Serbia. Their demands eventually led to the formation of the autonomous entity known as Republika Srpska in Bosnia and Herzegovina under the 1995 Dayton Agreement, which marked the end of the war.

Old Yugoslavia had now dissolved into five countries, with Serbia forming a federation with Montenegro—a short-lived union that was to last only until the Montenegrins voted for separation in 2006. This much-reduced "Federal Yugoslavia" was subject to rigorous UN sanctions under the charge that its government was responsible for war crimes during the Bosnian and Croatian conflicts. Sanctions led to further economic decline, and inflation reached more than 24,000 percent in one year alone, the prices of goods changing daily and wage packets becoming worthless soon after distribution.

Kosovo

The last of the regional wars took place in 1998–9, when Milošević directed Yugoslav military and security forces against Kosovan separatist guerillas, the Kosovo Liberation Army (KLA). The KLA had been intensifying guerilla attacks on the Serb public and police as a response to perceived Serb repression of the Albanian population.

Believing that the Yugoslav army was committing genocide against ethnic Albanians, and with the Western media talking up stories of atrocities, NATO forces entered the conflict to wage an air war on Yugoslavia, mostly concentrating on Serbia. Led by US General Wesley Clark, the bombing campaign lasted from the end of March to mid-June 1999, and launched around 38,000 sorties. As well as military targets, "dual-use" facilities such as bridges, factories, power stations, and—controversially—the Serbian television headquarters were also targeted. The fact that private factories were spared and only state-

owned factories bombed (unsurprisingly, some had been converted to weapons plants) fueled suspicion that the campaign was designed to lead the way for subsequent liberalization of the economy and prepare the ground for an influx of foreign capital.

Nevertheless, the bombing campaign came under harsh criticism in some quarters for the heavy destruction of civilian infrastructure and for inaccurate bombing by the so-called "precision weapons" (whether by mistake or design, including the Chinese Embassy in Belgrade). It was later observed that atrocities and killings appeared to increase massively rather than decrease after the onset of the bombing campaign.

When Milošević was forced to abandon his antiseparatist campaign in Kosovo, NATO entered the province in the form of the peacekeeping force KFOR. Kosovo's push for separation continued with a massive exodus of Serb refugees leaving the province for a new life in Serbia proper.

Subsequently, Kosovo was placed under transitional UN administration. During the years that followed, the international community tried and failed to reach an agreement on the future status of Kosovo. It was not until February 2008 that the Republic of Kosovo proclaimed its independence—naturally, not recognized by Serbia, and with mixed recognition from other countries, some wary of provoking their own separatist factions.

The International Criminal Tribunal for the former Yugoslavia (ICTY) was set up in The Hague to deal with war crimes from the 1990s conflicts. It indicted a number of people from Croatia, Bosnia,

Serbia, and Kosovo, including common soldiers, army generals, police commanders, and even the Croatian President Franjo Tudjman (who died just as the prosecution planned to indict him)—and the Serbian prime minister Slobodan Milošević.

The Bulldozer Revolution and the Return to Democracy

When the League of Communists dissolved in 1990, a multiparty system was introduced, the first time in history that the Serbian people had tasted democracy. A broad range of small political parties came into existence to challenge the leading Socialist Party of Serbia. However, in 1996 massive protests erupted in Belgrade over accusations that the Socialist Party had won the local elections fraudulently.

During the 2000 general elections Milošević was again accused of electoral fraud, causing widespread civil unrest and street demonstrations. He was compelled to concede defeat in what became known as the "Bulldozer Revolution." Milošević was arrested by Serbian forces in 2001 on charges of corruption and abuse of power, and afterward transferred to UN custody in Bosnia and finally to the ICTY, where he was on put on trial until his death in 2006.

Milošević had suffered from high blood pressure and his death was caused by a heart attack, but many in Serbia believe his trial to be an example of "victor's justice," and maintain that health care was not adequately provided for him in prison—or, indeed, that he was poisoned, either by the authorities or by his own hand.

The end of the Milošević era saw Serbia lose its international pariah status and start the process of European integration, which was declared a strategic priority. In 2007, the International Court of Justice in The Hague (set up to deal with states, not individuals) cleared Serbia of all charges of genocide, while still accepting that genocide perpetrated by individuals had taken place.

Serbia joined NATO's Partnership for Peace (PfP) in December 2006 and agreed to its first Individual Partnership Program (IPP) with NATO in 2009.

Serbia applied for European Union membership

on December 22, 2009. However, the conflict between conservative nationalist forces and reformist pro-EU forces still forms the sharpest division within domestic politics today.

THE ECONOMY

The currency of Serbia is the Serbian dinar (RSD). The dinar was first used in Serbia in the thirteenth century, although the modern dinar is a continuation of the Serbian dinar that dates back to 1867, the end of Ottoman influence in the region. In 2012 the exchange rate for €1.00 was about RSD 100, while the US $1.00 was about RSD 70. There are currently no plans to move toward the euro, even though the European Union is Serbia's largest trading partner.

The Serbian labor force consists of just over three million people, of whom more than half are employed in service industries. The remainder are employed in industry and agriculture.

Industry centers around metals, machinery, and furniture, as well as food production, textiles, chemicals, and pharmaceuticals. The machinery and higher-tech industries are concentrated in the main centers, Belgrade, Niš, and Novi Sad, and growth in these sectors attests to the high level of education of the workforce compared to its low wage base.

Another important sector is energy. Serbia exports almost half its energy production. Most energy is generated from hydroelectric and thermoelectric plants, and the growth of this sector is a precursor to general industrial growth in the country. Although Serbia's mineral wealth includes oil, natural gas, and coal, domestic oil production covers only about 10 percent of consumption.

The Serbian arms industry is significant, again closely linked to the metals and machinery sector and to a medium-to-high-tech infrastructure and skills base. During the Cold War, Yugoslavia was a large exporter of arms to the nonaligned countries, in particular North African states and various Arab countries. After a period of inactivity following the collapse of the republic, the sector is now in resurgence, with former business partnerships and contracts being renewed.

Agricultural production consists of wheat, corn, sugar beet, hemp, flax, and sunflower, as well as pork, beef, and milk. Serbia is also a large producer of fruit, especially plums and raspberries, and has extensive vineyards. Agricultural production is mainly concentrated in the flatlands of Vojvodina, and a large part of the agricultural economy is localized, consisting of small cooperatives and individual local farms. This explains why agriculture makes up only approximately 13 percent of GDP.

Decentralized, small-scale agricultural production gives rise to individuals producing their own wines, spirits, and cured meats and salamis—the Serbs are enthusiastic and proud pork farmers—hence the prevalence of "domestic" (homemade) produce in the market. Even city dwellers commonly own small vegetable patches not far from the cities, producing goods for themselves, their families, and their friends to help with the ever-increasing cost of living.

Export commodities consist of iron and steel, clothes, food, live animals, manufactured goods, machinery, arms, and transportation equipment. Serbia's main export partners are Italy, Bosnia and Herzegovina, and Germany, as well as neighboring Montenegro, Romania, and Macedonia. The key import partners are Russia, Germany, Italy, China, and Hungary, and major investor countries include Austria, Greece, Norway, Germany, and Italy.

Serbia's economy has been in transition since the late 1980s, when it moved from a Communist-style planned economy to a Western-style free-market model. Economic sanctions and war between 1992 and 1995 then delayed further growth and development, and hyperinflation (in fact, the highest inflation ever recorded in the world) destroyed the value of the dinar. To compound matters, the NATO bombings of 1999 targeted, among other things, state-owned factories and infrastructure. By 1999, the Serbian economy, infrastructure, and industry were only half the size they had been in 1990.

With the ousting of Milošević in 2000, economic liberalization started in earnest. Serbia rejoined the IMF, the World Bank, and the European Bank for Reconstruction and Development, and is working actively toward EU and WTO membership. In the last ten years GDP per capita has more than quadrupled, bringing higher standards of living but also an increasing trade deficit. In the same period, public debt has steadily decreased. The average wage in Serbia is approximately €500 per month, with pensions often less than two-thirds of this. Serbia has a weakened labor movement, with minimal health and safety laws and no minimum wage regulation. Unemployment is as high as 19 percent, and further investment in the private sector is sorely needed.

On the positive side, Serbia has a lot going for it— a very favorable and strategic location for trade and business within Europe, and between Europe and the Near East, and a rich history of international commerce. It also has a relatively inexpensive and highly educated labor force, and an increasingly sophisticated and demanding domestic market.

However, the Serbian economy faces many challenges, including lack of foreign investment, unemployment, a large trade deficit, and also an inefficient judicial system and high levels of corruption. It is a transitional economy, with unfinished privatization programs and incomplete structural reforms.

chapter two

VALUES & ATTITUDES

SERBIAN CULTURE

The richness and diversity of Serbian culture owes much to foreign invasions and occupations over the years. The Roman and Byzantine Empires, Greek missionaries, the Republic of Venice, and for over four centuries the Ottoman Empire, have all in one way or another both suppressed "indigenous" Serbian culture and shaped it into what we see today.

In recent times, in the Socialist Federal Republic of Yugoslavia, socialism was the predominant cultural stimulus. Today, however, Serbia is moving into a period where socialist ideas are being rejected: on the one hand, the younger generation looks toward presocialist Serbian culture and their identity as Slavic peoples within the Orthodox Church, an attempt perhaps to make sense of the difficult disintegration of the republic; and on the other hand, it looks toward the West, because of the ubiquity of Western culture and the supposed advantages that might be gained from joining the European project— its liberal democracy, higher standard of living, freedom of travel, and other benefits.

The diversity of Serbian culture can be seen in all aspects of national life—traditional dress, regional dialects, food, music, and literature. However, there is a bedrock of core values that truly unites the Serbian people.

RELIGION

Religion has always played a defining role in the history of the Serbs. From the early days of Serb settlement in the region, a succession of invading powers suppressed or otherwise influenced the indigenous religion, and this constant reshaping of the religious landscape continues to this day.

The main religion of Serbia is Serbian Orthodox Christianity, which is practiced by 84 percent of the population. Serbs became Christian under the Byzantine Empire from the seventh to the ninth century, but it was not until the thirteenth century that Rastko Nemanjić, later named St. Sava, formed the Serbian Orthodox Church. An independent Church, it ranks sixth in order of seniority of the Orthodox Churches after those of Constantinople, Alexandria, Antioch, Jerusalem, and Russia. Serbian Orthodoxy is also practiced in the surrounding regions by 74 percent of the population of Montenegro, 36 percent in Bosnia and Herzegovina, and 4.4 percent in Croatia.

St. Sava is the most prominent figure in the Serbian religion, and has a cathedral named after him in Belgrade, built on the site where the Ottomans burned his remains in the eighteenth century. This glorious place of worship is one of the largest Orthodox cathedrals in the world.

Serbian Orthodox churches and cathedrals are Byzantine in style, with a rectangular foundation supporting a major dome in the center surrounded by smaller domes to the sides. Inside, the walls and ceilings are enriched by frescoes and paintings of scenes from the Bible and Christian tradition. Churches are some of the most impressive buildings in Serbia and are often set in areas of outstanding natural beauty.

However, Serbia's religious history began hundreds of years before the Byzantine conversion, when the native religion was paganism and polytheism. A remnant of this can be found today in eastern Serbia, among an ethnic minority group called the Vlachs. Vlachs are of Roman origin and have managed to preserve their traditions and culture, along with their original Latin-based language, although it is not used in local administration. Assimilated into the Orthodox Christian Church in the nineteenth century, the Vlachs are an example of an ethnic group living in Serbia that has stayed in touch with its pagan traditions. They continue to practice their pre-Christian religious customs to this day.

Serbia today is a multireligious country. Roman Catholicism is practiced by 6 percent of the population, mostly in the northern part of

Vojvodina, by members of local ethnic groups such as Hungarians, Croats, Germans, Roma, Bunjevi, and Rusyns. Protestant Christianity is also practiced in Serbia among the ethnic Slovaks, as well as by some Hungarians and Germans. Various Protestant groups, including Methodists, Evangelical Baptists, and Seventh-day Adventists, can be found in the province of Vojvodina.

With the arrival of the Ottoman Empire in the fourteenth and fifteenth centuries many Serbs, mostly living in Bosnia, converted to Islam. Today in Serbia, Islam is practiced by 5 percent of the population, mostly in the southern part of the country around Raška, Preševo, Bujanovac, and the disputed province of Kosovo. Bosniaks, Albanians, Turks, Arabs, and Egyptians are the ethnic groups currently practicing Islam in Serbia.

Jews arrived in Serbia in Roman times in small numbers, and later in much bigger numbers when fleeing the Spanish and Portuguese inquisitions, when they were welcomed by the Ottoman Empire and allowed to flourish. Their presence in the region was almost completely wiped out during the turmoil of the two world wars, and especially during the Nazi occupation of the region.

Religion continues to play an important role in Serbian daily life. The religious calendar is filled with a profusion of saints' days, celebrated by families in the traditional way—often involving a visit to church, prayers, and the lighting of candles. On these and other important days priests will make a house visit, and pilgrimages to cathedrals and monasteries are still a popular social activity for young and old alike.

FAMILY VALUES

The Serbian family is based upon patriarchal values. The father is the head of the household and makes all the important decisions concerning the family unit. In rural Serbia, large patriarchal families are still dominant, and it is important to have male heirs to continue the family name.

Traditionally, Serbs are loyal and devoted to their extended families, and extended family members offer assistance and resources throughout life. Family relationships are close, so, for example, first and second cousins are referred to as brothers and sisters, rather than cousins as in the West. The language reflects these relationships and has precise terminology defining them. The distinctions reflected in these terms have no exact equivalent in English. Some examples are given below.

> *stric* (uncle—father's brother)
> *ujak* (uncle—mother's brother)
> *svastika* (sister-in-law—wife's sister)
> *zaova* (sister-in-law—husband's sister)
> *surak* (brother-in-law—wife's brother)
> *dever* (brother-in-law—husband's brother)

Within the extended family, marriage is not allowed between relatives even down to seven-times-removed cousins—such a relationship would still be considered incestuous.

Parents are expected to provide support for their children well beyond their twenty-first birthday, and commonly until they can stand on their own feet in life. The ideas of independence and individuality so prized in the West are less important here. Children are not as keen to flee the family nest and branch out on their own as they are in the West, and economic conditions also preclude this behavior.

Parents usually provide newly married couples with housing, either by helping them buy or build a new home, or by sharing their own living quarters. Often, parents will build a new story on top of their house to accommodate their offspring, so it is not uncommon to have two or three generations living under the same roof, although often with separate entrances in order to maintain some privacy.

Equally, children traditionally look after their aged parents. Placing one's parents in a nursing home is not acceptable. To a Serb, the idea of a nursing home outside the family is intolerable: "If the children won't look after me, this means that I have failed as a parent and the children are paying me back."

Yet, like many parts of the world, modern Serbia is starting to suffer from what is known as the "white plague" *(bela kuga)*—the perceived consequences of Western imported independence, individuality, and urban living, which acts to erode the traditional culture. Young couples are afraid to enter into marriage: they are marrying less and later in life, are divorcing more often, and have fewer children, thus allowing themselves to pursue ambitions outside the family. Couples are also having children without marrying first, although this is still taboo in the more conservative parts of the country. This conflict between traditional and modern values is not confined to Serbia.

THE ROLE OF WOMEN

The Serbian woman is traditionally the hardworking pillar of the family. An exemplary wife, daughter, and mother, she often holds down a full-time job outside the home. This cultural shift was established over many years of conflict when women were forced to work in traditional male roles while the men were away fighting.

The end of the Second World War saw Tito extend full rights to women: equal education, employment, and social and political standing. Women, however, continue to take on all the household and child-rearing duties, with the husband there to help only at critical moments of the children's development.

The Serbian woman is typically proud of her beauty and has a vain streak (witness the silicon-enhanced augmentations of the Belgrade *nouveaux riches*). She dresses to kill, while simultaneously taking great pride in her cooking expertise, her domestic proficiency, and her dedication as a mother.

International Women's Day on March 8, marking the economic, political, and social achievements of women, is an important event in Serbia. It is widely celebrated, with women being acknowledged by their friends, colleagues, and employers—for example, it is common to give roses to female coworkers and friends, and the simple greeting *"Sretan dan žena"* ("Happy Women's Day") is a must.

PRIDE AND HONOR

Personal and collective pride and honor are important values in Serbian culture. "Saving pride" (*sačuvati ponos*) is a topic discussed as a matter of everyday discourse, and especially in relation to any national achievement in the political sphere—but it is also a ubiquitous topic at the social level.

People take great pride in the work they do and the produce they create. So, for example, when Serbian hosts offer their homemade spirit, *loza*, to their guests, or a salad of tomatoes and cucumbers grown in the garden, they will certainly expect their efforts to be acknowledged! This should not be a problem: the local produce and domestically distilled spirits are generally of the highest quality, and a real treat for those used to mass-produced, supermarket fare.

It would be a matter of pride and honor that the man of the house perform the "masculine" duties of building, repairing, fixing the electricity, and plumbing, whereas the more "feminine" duties of housekeeping and child rearing would be a matter of pride for the woman of the house, with very little crossover of these responsibilities in a traditional household. The man who does not know the basics of DIY, or the woman who does not know how to cook, is a rarity in Serbia.

A man's manners are closely observed, and it is expected that men will do the physical tasks such as heavy lifting, including carrying a woman's shopping bags (for women who are known to him). A man would be expected to hold the door open for a woman, or to give up his seat on the bus. Similarly, men are always expected to pick up the bill for their female companion when eating or drinking one-to-one in a café or restaurant.

SOCIAL INTOLERANCE

Although Serbian society is generally progressive, lesbian, gay, bisexual, and transgender (LGBT) rights still fall behind those in the rest of Europe. Homosexual activity is legal in Serbia, but it is a cultural taboo, and prejudice is still prevalent, especially among far-right and nationalistic groups. Same-sex couples have no standing in law, and marriage is defined as the union between a man and a woman. However, antidiscrimination laws do exist to protect these minorities.

Gay bashing occurs, most notably at the Belgrade Gay Pride marches over the last few years. However, the tide is turning and politicians have shown up on recent marches to lend their support against intolerance. There are gay scenes in Belgrade, Novi Sad, and Subotica, with a number of clubs, venues, and bars friendly to the subculture.

UNEXPECTED INTIMACY

The Serbs are fun-loving people, but a strong strain of self-pity is evident in their mentality. Conversations between friends or strangers will often stray into topics such as the poor standard of living, or poor job conditions. This sense of victimhood explains why people you have only just met may tell you in great detail about their ill health or lousy job prospects, for these are real problems that afflict Serbia after years of conflict and economic isolation.

However, this attitude is also indicative of the emotionally open and generous Balkan character. A visitor from a more phlegmatic culture may well be taken aback at such immediate intimacy, but will soon warm to the generosity of spirit that it reveals.

HOSPITALITY AND GENEROSITY

Serbs are great hosts, and hospitality is highly regarded. When a visitor enters a Serbian home, the host (normally the man of the house) will go out of his way to offer whatever the visitor may want—a shot of *loza*, for example, or a plate of the best produce available. It is important to offer "the best"— as well as the best food and drink, this might also mean the best room of the house, even if it is the host's own room.

The Serbian house is generally arranged around a large reception area, often open-plan to the kitchen and with a dining table. In rural areas where more space is available, an outdoor kitchen and dining terrace will also be found. This emphasis on eating, drinking, and entertaining is a key element of the Serbian identity, and forms the backbone to many social rituals, such as the Slava or the communal meals that accompany weddings and funerals.

When a large group is drinking in a bar or dining at a restaurant, it is still common for one member of the group to jump in and pay for the whole table— and sometimes a small conflict may ensue as rival hosts battle to get their wallets out first. For this reason the more discreet individual may surreptitiously sneak to the bar and settle the bill before anyone else has a chance! In this sense, there is more value to be gained in treating one's friends than in saving money.

It will be a matter of pride to the "host" in this situation that he or she is able to provide for others. The reverse is also true—the individual who always keeps his or her wallet closed will soon gain a bad reputation, unless it is common knowledge that they really can't afford it (which, with high unemployment in Serbia, is not uncommon). The best way to become known and liked in a group of Serbs is to make the odd grand gesture with the checkbook— and not offer to split the bill equally!

WORK ETHIC

Serbs are hardworking people. Arguably they have a much better handle on work–life balance than people in the West. Working hours generally start and finish early, so it is not uncommon to work from 8:00 a.m. to 3:00 p.m. and still have the afternoon free for socializing and family duties.

Although it is clear that the Serbs work hard to support their families, it often seems that some of the most important aspects of working life are coffee and cigarette breaks—especially in state-owned institutions, as anyone who has ever had to arrange a visa extension or pay a parking fine will attest.

The "efficiency" of the Western service sector has no parallel in Serbia, and a job that might take a couple of hours in London might take a couple of days in Belgrade. Those unfamiliar with the way things work will find themselves endlessly turning up at the wrong time—during breakfast hour, cigarette break, computer systems overhaul . . . or simply showing up too late. It is common for an institution to shut its doors to the public at 9: 00 a.m., meaning that you would have to stand in line from 6:00 a.m. to catch that small window of opportunity between 8:00 and 9:00 when someone is there to see you. In Serbia the only way to get a task done efficiently is to know someone from the inside, or *"ako imas vezu"* (if you have a connection). It is, after all, a culture that depends on close personal relationships.

COMMUNAL AND INDIVIDUAL SPIRIT

Almost half a century since the Tito era, the spirit of socialism is still very much present in Serbian culture. People often act together in large groups with an apparent "collective consciousness," the emphasis being on group, rather than individual, needs. A comparison with a big group of sports fans would be fair, and would go some way to explaining the popularity of team sports in modern Serbian culture. Anyone who has found themselves in central Belgrade after a win by the seemingly unimportant national handball team will understand.

Whereas in the West a large group of friends may quickly splinter into smaller subgroups on a night out, in Serbian culture it is important that the group "sticks together," and any attempt to break this may be seen as antisocial. Individualism is often regarded as a strange phenomenon imported from the West.

For example, people will speak about themselves in the plural rather than the singular. "Our mum is calling us for dinner" is a common expression even when other siblings are not present.

BRIBERY AND CORRUPTION

Bribery and corruption are present in all aspects of Serbian political and business life. In a way, the Communist regime encouraged acceptance of this culture. Although not massively totalitarian, the Party still operated a hierarchical rather than a meritocratic system, which created a culture of patronage.

To compound the issue, in the 1990s UN sanctions caused a shortage of imported products such as oil and medicine. In order to satisfy the basic needs of the populace, illegal (sanction-busting) trade had to be organized at the highest level. This top-down "corruption" affected everyone from government officials to small-time smugglers. Making illegal, lucrative deals for personal gain was necessary for the economy, so the accompanying system of kickbacks and payoffs became overt business practice.

Bribery is often a socially acceptable form of payment, although it is illegal. Paying your way to the top of the doctor's waiting list with coffee and chocolates is a common small bribe, as is paying part of your speeding fine in cash to the arresting officer—indeed, in some parts of the country the traffic police may stop vehicles deliberately to extract bribes from unsuspecting motorists, even if they have done nothing wrong. Of course, this behavior continues to be unexceptional while the average wages in Serbia are so low by European standards.

On a larger scale, and because of high levels of unemployment, people often have to "buy" their jobs. To secure a good state job, a potential employee may pay his or her future manager up to a whole year's salary. Again, this is just the cost of doing business. Having a personal connection, *vezu*, is often the only way to get something done without recourse to payoffs, and again emphasizes the importance of personal connections in Serbian culture.

URBAN–RURAL DIFFERENCES

Before the Second World War, Serbia had an agricultural economy based around small towns and villages, the larger cities being administrative centers of culture and finance.

After the war, the Communists encouraged migration to urban areas by creating employment for unskilled workers in the nascent industrial sector. The Communist leadership had little faith in the economic power of the agricultural peasantry, and hoped to achieve the preeminence of the working class through a modern industrial economy. They nationalized 80 percent of the land and ordered rapid industrialization, so the peasants left their farms to work in the new factories and offices.

Communism thus rendered the landowning peasantry a thing of the past; peasants were considered provincial, narrow-minded people, an embarrassment to forward-looking Communist

Yugoslavia. Even nowadays, calling someone *"seljak"* (villager) is a common insult.

With the disintegration of the Communist state, the political and economic depression of the 1990s, and the effects of the wars, the economic gap between rural and urban areas has grown wider.

Migration from country to city continues apace, and urban sprawl can be observed in areas around larger cities as well as around smaller towns such as Kragujevac, Niš, Užice, Novi Pazar, or Valjevo.

Most rural households live on an acutely low income, sourcing the basics of life from the local economy—from home produce, neighboring farms, and other smallholdings. Often rural families cannot afford to give their children a higher education. Even the mandatory national curriculum is frequently unaffordable, as the appropriate institutions are based in the towns, requiring children to commute by car or bus. Those who do manage to educate their children soon see them leave for better prospects in the cities, further eroding the rural community.

FOLKLORE AND SUPERSTITION

Before Orthodox Christianity took root, the Slavs held pagan beliefs, and many mythic and folkloric traditions endure to this day. Uncertainty about the future naturally prompts individuals to look to the past to make sense of the world. Serbs are a superstitious people and take their beliefs very seriously. Of course, there is a fine line between religious belief, folk wisdom, and superstition—and varying levels of truth to each.

Natural and folk cures are popular for common ailments—so garlic will fly off the shelves at the first sign of flu, and herbal teas and remedies will be offered for afflictions as varied as arthritis or indigestion. These remedies are part of a traditional culture handed down by word of mouth through the generations, something that has been stifled in the West by the advancement of scientific rationalism and pharmaceutical capitalism.

People with more serious problems, be they physical or emotional, may consult a "witch doctor." These doctors range from reputable but uncertified herbalists and osteopaths to alternative therapists and individuals with various levels of psychic ability. For the modern Serb such a consultation would be carried out as well as, not instead of, a visit to a conventional medical doctor. Even in present-day Belgrade witch doctors are surprisingly prevalent, and people will travel great distances to consult a doctor of reputation.

For example, a run of bad luck may have been caused by a jealous neighbor slipping a malignant object down the back of your sofa—the witch doctor will advise you where to find this object, and when you have removed it from your house your luck will turn.

chapter three

HOLIDAYS &
CELEBRATIONS

Working people in Serbia have on average twenty to
thirty days of annual leave. Serbs enjoy their holiday
times in groups, surrounded by extended family and
friends, so they often take their annual leave for
specific social events, rather than opting for far-flung
holidays in exotic locations.

Holidays commonly involve traveling to nearby
coastal regions during the swimming months, or
enjoying local ski resorts in the winter season.
Another popular holiday pastime, especially for the
older generation, is health tourism—the yearly visit
to the local spa. There are more than forty major
centers of these across the country.

"Ethno-villages" are also hugely popular getaways.
These villages are tourist destinations specifically
designed to give visitors a taste of traditional rural
life and allow guests to experience the simple life,
close to nature and removed from the pressures of
modern living.

Foreign travel has become popular only in recent
years, with economic growth and the opening up of
the market to the West. However, Serbia is still a long
way from the "budget airlines" culture enjoyed in
richer countries, and until recently visa restrictions

made foreign travel complicated, confining it to ex-Yugoslav republics and other neighboring countries.

PUBLIC HOLIDAYS
There are eight nonworking public holidays in Serbia, of which three relate to Orthodox Christianity:

2 days for New Year—January 1 and 2
1 day for Orthodox Christmas—January 7
1 day for National State Day—February 15
2 days for Orthodox Easter—Good Friday and Easter Monday (dates vary)
2 days for Workers' Day—May 1 and 2

Serbia follows the same business calendar as the West (the Gregorian calendar). However, the religious year is based upon the old Julian calendar, making celebrations such as Christmas around fourteen days adrift of the Gregorian calendar.

Government offices, businesses, schools, and universities will be closed on these days. The only exception is the service sector supplying food and drink, so if in you are in Belgrade during a public holiday, you will not be able to do business or shop, but you will be able to eat and drink as usual.

In addition to public holidays, religious groups have the right to additional days off on their respective religious holidays, which are not counted as annual leave days. These holidays might affect businesses where a minority group is prevalent, but mostly go unnoticed.

These days include one day for Orthodox Christians celebrating Slava; one day for Catholics celebrating Christmas, and two extra days for the Catholic Easter; one day at the beginning and one day at the end of Ramadan for Muslims; and one day at Yom Kippur for Jews.

PUBLIC HOLIDAY CELEBRATIONS
New Year

New Year is celebrated extensively across Serbia. From late December cities are illuminated and decorated, and remain so until late January while Julian calendar festivities are still under way.

Families celebrate New Year's Eve indoors with a New Year tree (*novogodisnja jelka*), equivalent to the Christmas tree in the West. There is an abundance of food and drink, prepared in advance and enjoyed over the next few days, and children believe that Father Christmas (*Deda Mraz*, "Father Frost") will arrive at around midnight to deliver presents under the tree.

In major cities such as Belgrade, Novi Sad, and Niš, going out on New Year's Eve is the major attraction. New Year is a time for outdoor festivities—open-air parties, concerts in the city squares, and mass gatherings in public areas. Fireworks mark midnight, and concerts and parties continue into the early hours.

Popular restaurants, clubs, cafés, and hotels celebrate with food and live music, and are often booked up in advance. And, as if that wasn't enough, the first evening of the new year is also a big going-out night, with partygoers looking for a repeat of the previous night's extravagance, many having partied all day!

On the first day of the year, the central street in Belgrade is closed to traffic; music, entertainment, and open-air theater are performed in a carnival atmosphere, with food and warm drink served to help with the often subzero temperatures. Individuals, families, celebrities, and politicians—sometimes including the president—come out to walk in the streets and do their bit for the festival.

Orthodox Christmas

Christmas is the most celebrated holiday in Serbia. The customs surrounding it are complex, and locals often discuss these at length to ensure they are following the correct rules.

Christmas day falls on January 7, but celebrations begin the night before on Christmas Eve *(Badnji Dan)*. Early in the morning, the men of the household announce their departure by firing guns into the air, as they go out to choose the *badnjak* or Yule log, a suitable tree branch to be burned inside the house that evening. Prayers are said before cutting the branches, which are decorated with dry leaves and twigs. City dwellers can buy their *badnjak* in the markets and on the street.

Before Christmas Eve dinner, the men bring their *badnjak* into the house; the women greet them at the door by throwing grains over them. The logs are added to a fire or stove, and the family spreads straw over the floor. This straw remains in place for several

days, and is often kept in storage for other rituals that might require it during the year.

Christmas Eve dinner is a rich and elaborate affair, but is prepared in accordance with the Orthodox rules of fasting—so, generally vegan in style (no cheese, milk, or eggs) with the exception of fish. After dinner, people gather outside their local church, where each family brings one extra *badnjak* to burn on the church bonfire. Drinks such as mulled wine and hot *rakija* (homemade brandy) are served, and the church rings its bells at midnight, often accompanied by additional gunfire.

On the morning of Christmas Day there will be a well-attended service in church. The women of the house get up early to collect fresh water from the local spring, named "strong water" *(jaka voda)*; city women collect this water from church. The whole family washes their faces with this water, for purity and good health, and the water is used to bake the Christmas bread, in which a gold coin is hidden for one lucky winner.

The first person to visit the house on Christmas Day is considered an auspicious guest, called the *polaznik*. The *polaznik* is believed to bring good luck and health for the whole year, and this visitor is often preselected, young children who are considered pure and free from evil often being invited.

In rural areas, men spit roast a pig or sheep for Christmas lunch, the richest and most festive meal of the year, involving copious amounts of food and drink. A lamb or pork roast (or both) normally suffices for city dwellers. The head of the house starts the dinner celebrations by lighting a candle, burning frankincense, and saying a prayer. Family members will stand up to kiss each other and wish each other Happy Christmas, and then everyone together holds the Christmas bread with both hands and rotates it fully three times before each breaks a piece off for themselves. A piece is saved for any absent family member.

Gifts are not exchanged at Serbian Christmas. Instead, on the three Sundays prior to Christmas, presents are given by the children, then by mothers, and then by fathers, consecutively. These gifts are given as a ransom for being captured—for example, on the day that mothers give presents, children have to capture their mother and tie her to a table or tree.

To gain her freedom, the mother must tell them where she has hidden her presents for them. Likewise, the children must do this to their father on a separate day, and the parents must tie up their children on the day when it is their turn to give presents.

For the next few days of Christmas, families traditionally visit relatives and friends, the Christmas period lasting fourteen days in total.

Easter

Easter is the holiest day of the year for Orthodox Christians, marking Christ's resurrection from the dead with a sumptuous feast. In Serbia, the exact date of Easter is calculated according to the Julian calendar, corresponding to rules set down by the Orthodox Church, so this date seldom coincides with the Western Easter—and, like the Western Easter, the date changes every year.

Serbs observe Lent for forty-eight days, starting on a day known as "Clean Monday" *(Čisti ponedeljak)*. The fasting period includes the six Sundays before Easter. Those observing Lent abstain from eating meat, dairy products, and eggs, and often wine and oil too. Younger people, or those less inclined to observe the full fasting period, might choose to fast for a shorter seven-day period, or maybe only on Good Friday.

Easter eggs are important to the Serbian Easter tradition. On the Thursday before Easter hens' eggs

are hard-boiled and painted with natural dyes, such as red onionskin, orange and lemon peel, or yellow turmeric. Elaborately painted floral patterns are created with the help of wax, or sometimes scratched onto the surface with a sharp tool. Although any color may be used, some eggs must be dyed red to symbolize the resurrection.

The first egg to be boiled and decorated is a red egg named *"Čuvarkuća,"* meaning "home protector." This egg will be saved until the following Easter, when it is buried outside in the ground near the house.

The rest of the eggs are presented in a basket, often blessed by the local priest, and then served up for breakfast on Easter Sunday. Before eating, everyone takes part in the egg-tapping contest. In this traditional game each player chooses a painted egg, then players pair off and proceed to tap their eggs together to see which cracks first. A series of heats determines the winner, who is the one whose egg is intact at the end of the game, and who is said to have good luck. The losers are forced to eat their own cracked eggs.

An early morning liturgy starts outside the church on Easter Sunday. The priest blesses all those waiting for the service, while he chants, holding a cross and candle in one hand and a thurible or censer containing burning frankincense in the other. Only after this ritual will he open the doors of the church for the service to start.

Easter lunch is served later in the day, and like all Serbian celebratory meals is rich and diverse, with traditional recipes. The meal starts with a chicken or lamb soup *(čorba)*, to be followed by spit-roasted lamb or pork and *sarma* (stuffed cabbage), not forgetting the numerous cured meats, salads, vegetables, breads, cheeses, and pastries, all washed down with red wine.

THE SLAVA

Slava, the celebration of the feast day of a family's patron saint, is the biggest event of the year for a Serbian family. On this day, the family opens its doors to friends and relations, welcoming them with the best food and drink.

The origins of Slava date back to when the Serbs were polytheistic pagan tribes. In those times, each household had its own protective god, who was venerated with an annual feast. This tradition was later assimilated into Serbian Orthodoxy with Christian saints replacing the old Slavic deities. Nowadays every Serbian family has its own patron saint, but there are differing opinions as to how these saints were originally chosen. One theory has it that the date of their conversion to Christianity (the first baptism) determined the family saint, whereas others believe it was a simple swap from an old pagan god to an equivalent Christian saint.

The patron saint is inherited though the paternal line, passed on to all sons. Hence, related families that share a surname celebrate Slava at the same time. Daughters celebrate their father's Slava only until they marry, at which point they start celebrating their husband's saint day.

Traditionally, extended families lived in large households under the same roof, so, as long as the family patriarch was alive, the whole extended family celebrated together. In recent times, with increasing migration to the cities and atomization of the extended family, a son must ask permission from his father to celebrate in his own home.

The Slava is an exclusively Serbian tradition, celebrated even by atheists as a hereditary family holiday, a mark of cultural identity. The Serbs have a saying: "Where there is a Slava, there is a Serb."

Although the Slava is not a public holiday, because the date differs depending on the saint, individuals can take an extra day's holiday for the celebration, not counted in their annual leave. Because it involves elaborate cooking and house preparations that take several days of work, many Serbian women take a whole week off to prepare for it.

On the day of Slava, the local priest will come to the home to conduct a small service: a blessing of the house, family members, and the food and drink on offer. He also lights the blessed Slava candle and sometimes performs a memorial for dead relatives. A festive lunch or dinner is served later that day for the many guests, with a sumptuous formal meal prepared in accordance with religious observance: on Wednesdays and Fridays it is usual to serve only fish and vegetarian dishes; on all other days numerous cured, boiled, and roasted meats will be offered, along with salads, soups, *sarma*, and so on. The meal consists of many courses, and it is advisable for the uninitiated to pace themselves in order to sample everything on offer.

Traditionally, *slavski kolač* (the Slava cake) is served. This cake is actually closer to bread; it is made with boiled wheat, walnuts, and honey, and decorated with the cross.

The most celebrated of the Orthodox saints in Serbia are St. Nicholas, St. George, St. John the Baptist, St. Sava, and St. Vitus, and accordingly their feast days are the most common Slava days.

WEDDINGS

Weddings in Serbia are famously high-spirited occasions, filled with music, dancing, food, and drink.

There are still people alive who have experienced arranged marriages, but nowadays most nuptials are love matches. However, it is still traditional for the groom to ask the bride's father for his daughter's hand, even though he is unlikely to be refused. Each family then organizes its own pre-wedding celebration centered on food, drink, and live music.

On the morning of the wedding, the groom's entourage will walk en masse to the bride's home. Along with the groom's father, brothers and uncles, other important members of this group include the *kum* (best man) and the *barjaktar* (flag bearer), who walks in front of the group carrying a flag (commonly the national flag), and later in front of the bridal car from her house to the church. If the bride's family live far away, the group will arrive the night before in order to start the proceedings early the next morning.

The groom's party must barter for the bride's hand. On arrival at the bride's home, the groom waits outside while his entourage offers various presents to the family, including money, until a deal is struck. The father or brothers of the bride will often offer up bridesmaids first if a suitable price is not suggested. This negotiation may have started prior to the wedding day, and can vary from a purely symbolic ritual to a serious arrangement, depending on the financial standing of the families involved.

When the bride has finally been "bought" and handed over, she will be taken to the church where other guests are already waiting. The bride is often serenaded by a band before she enters the church.

The couple say their vows and exchange wedding rings, and are blessed by the priest. They are then crowned by the priest, signifying becoming the king and the queen of their own kingdom, the marital home. The couple then stand together while the guests file past them, kissing the bride and groom on each cheek and shaking hands, wishing them a happy life together.

As they leave the church, the best man tosses coins—rather than confetti—into the air, symbolizing luck and future prosperity. Only children are allowed to pick up the coins, and they compete to collect the most. The wedding band will be waiting outside, and soon the whole wedding party will be dancing a *kolo*, a traditional folk dance where everyone stands in a circle, holding hands, dancing from the hips to a rhythmic, fast-paced beat.

The party moves to the reception, where the guests will eat, drink, and exchange presents until no one is left standing. You are unlikely to go

hungry or thirsty at a Serbian wedding, for parties typically offer a rich menu, endless amounts of alcohol, and live music entertainment.

Gypsy trumpeters always make an appearance, sometimes uninvited, adding a touch of madness to an already festive atmosphere. They will blow their trumpets at anyone willing to throw money into their instruments, moving from guest to guest as partygoers compete for their attention. The party will continue with *kolo* dancing, favorite wedding songs, and increasing inebriation. The couple will leave for their marital home in the early evening, leaving their guests to party into the night.

BIRTH

After a birth, traditionally mother and child don't leave the house for forty days. During this time the child will not receive visitors, and those wishing to see it must come to the *babine* (the first visit to the newborn), six weeks after birth. This is to guard the baby from the "evil eye" and from external influences such as dirt, bacteria, and viruses; however, many young couples today are relaxed about this rule.

Traditionally, baby and mother move to the maternal grandparents' house when the forty-day period is over. It used to be customary for newlyweds to live with the husband's parents, the birth of a child prompting a change of household so that the maternal grandparents can acquaint themselves with the baby, and allowing the new mother to learn skills from her own mother.

After six weeks, people will continue to visit the household to celebrate the baby's arrival. The uncles, aunts, and other close relatives of the newborn may also receive visitors, as Serbs welcome any excuse for a celebration. Visitors will bring a small present for the parents and will tuck some money under the baby's mattress or pillow. An old Serbian tradition has it that arriving guests rip or tear the father's or grandfather's shirt, for luck.

For religious families, baptism happens at least forty days after birth, and often much later. The baptism ceremony is an intimate affair, with only close friends and family present. After full immersion in holy water, the baby is anointed with olive oil to welcome him or her to the Holy Spirit. The priest then cuts three locks of hair from the child's head: symbolic of strength and an expression of gratitude to God, as the child has nothing else to give. The godparents hold the baby during the ceremony, and they are normally the *kumovi* (best man and maid of honor) from the wedding.

FUNERALS

In Serbia funerals follow a strict protocol. The deceased is presented in an open coffin in his or her home, and is buried within twenty-four hours of death—or forty-eight if relatives have to travel great distances to the funeral. In cities, and some smaller towns, it is common to use the chapel instead of the home. Elsewhere, the house of the deceased is transformed into a chapel: one room is made available for the coffin, which is placed on a table in the center, and the walls are lined with chairs.

The death is publicized in an *osmrtnice*, or death notice, attached to various designated places in the area, such as bulletin boards outside workplaces or bus stops. These are small obituary flyers, with black borders and a picture of the deceased, announcing the time and place of the funeral. If the deceased was Christian, the *osmrtnice* will contain a cross; if the deceased was a Communist, then a five-pointed star will feature instead.

In the past—and still in some rural areas—it was important to inform every house in the village of the death, and a messenger would knock on each door and say the same words without entering into the house or engaging in further conversation. Nowadays, the mobile phone and the posting of *osmrtnices* perform much the same function.

Soon after death, the deceased is bathed by older relatives, dressed in a new suit, and placed in a coffin with some favorite belongings, such as jewelry, coffee, cigarettes, or money. The dead person must not be left alone even for one moment, so friends and relatives sit with the body all day and night. Since people come to the house to offer condolences over this twenty-four-hour period, there is a continuous assortment of visitors coming and going.

With religious families, the priest comes to the house just before the funeral to conduct prayers, before a bigger service later in church. The funeral procession then walks from the house to the church and the cemetery; a large cross is carried in front of the coffin, followed by the immediate family and the rest of the mourners. At nonreligious funerals the procedure is much the same, except that the procession will bypass the church and walk straight to the cemetery.

In some parts of the country musicians head the procession, playing songs written specifically for funerals. These orchestras might consist of anything from a small folk band to a twenty-piece brass band. It is sometimes customary for the women of the family to weep loudly—almost singing—during the funeral, creating an atmosphere of melancholy and sorrow. When the women of the family don't know how to weep in this way, the family pays another woman to perform the task for them.

After the church service, speeches are made at the graveside before the coffin is lowered into the ground. In past times, and even today in some parts of southern Serbia, a white bedsheet was placed on the grave once the coffin had been lowered and covered with earth, and various foods were placed on top to be offered to the mourners, who were obliged to eat something.

Mourners are offered a spoonful of boiled wheat and a shot of spirit on leaving the cemetery. One must not leave the cemetery without washing one's hands, so there are always washbasins by the exit.

After the funeral the mourners share a meal to celebrate the life of the deceased. This meal is prepared in accordance with local customs (no cured, baked, or fried foods), and is a chance for relatives and friends to remember their loved one in an informal setting. The meal is served at the house of the deceased or in a local restaurant, but not all mourners present at the funeral are invited—invitations are made on a more personal basis by the family.

Close relatives of the deceased will mourn for a whole year, but there is a shorter mourning period of forty days during which they will constantly receive visitors to their homes. These visitors will often bring a small gift such as coffee and cookies.

Close relatives observe remembrance days by getting together, visiting the grave and placing flowers on it, and eating a meal. This is done seven days after the death, then at forty days, and then each year thereafter on the anniversary of the death. The forty-day period is especially important, as Serbs believe that during this time a person's soul travels around this world before departing. For this reason, it is important to keep one window in the house open during this period so the soul can easily return, and not to touch, rearrange, or wash any of the dead person's clothes or possessions. The fear is that the deceased might not recognize their home and might not be present at the forty-day parting ceremony, so that the soul might wander off without finding peace in the world.

Women in mourning observe strict clothing customs, dressing completely in black for a period of time dictated by their closeness to the deceased. Immediate family, such as wife, sister, daughter, or daughter-in-law, will wear black for a whole year. More distant relatives might wear black for forty days only, while others might wear it only at the funeral. It is considered bad manners to wear any makeup or jewelry at funerals, although mostly only family members observe this. The mourning period does not have rules only for clothing—during this period, the mourners will not make house visits to their friends or attend any sort of celebration.

IMPORTANT RELIGIOUS DATES
The Red-Letter Days and the Calendar

Every Serbian household keeps a copy of the religious calendar in the form of a small booklet containing descriptions of all the existing saints, the dates when they are celebrated, and a conversion table from the Julian to the Gregorian calendar. The highest-ranking saints and Sundays are marked in red. Most Serbs observe *Crvena Svola*, or red-letter days, as nonworking days, referring to household chores (excluding cooking) rather than to employment.

Serbian New Year, or "*Srpska Nova Godina*"

This is celebrated according to the Julian calendar, on January 14. Although a working day, on this day, and also on the night before on New Year's Eve, small-scale celebrations are held across the country resembling those of the Gregorian New Year two weeks earlier.

St. Sava

St. Sava was a Serbian prince, diplomat, and monk, and became the first archbishop of the Serbian Church in 1219. He is considered one of the most important figures in Serbian history, and many mark his day, January 27, by going to churches dedicated to him. St. Sava was the founder of Serbian law and literature, and hence became the patron saint of schools. So, although St. Sava's Day is a working day, most schools will have no lessons but instead a series of workshops and activities in honor of the saint.

St. Vitus or Vidovdan

Also known as "*Svetovid*," this is a working day, but has long been considered a date of special

importance to ethnic Serbs. Svetovid was the much-honored pagan Slavic god of war, who was transformed into St. Vitus during the Christianization of the Serbs in the ninth century. On St. Vitus's Day in 1389 the Battle of Kosovo against the

Ottoman Empire took place, and the Serbian knight Miloš Obilić killed Sultan Murad I. Subsequently, but not coincidentally, St. Vitus's Day 1914 saw the assassination of Archduke Franz Ferdinand in Sarajevo, triggering the First World War. A variety of other important events concerning Serbia happened on this day—for example, the signing of the Treaty of Versailles in 1919, the creation of the first constitution of the Kingdom of Serbs, Croats, and Slovenes in 1921, and the deportation of Slobodan Milošević in 2001 to the ICTY in The Hague. These important events are remembered on June 28 across the country and celebrated with passion and patriotism.

chapter four

MAKING
FRIENDS

SERBIAN FRIENDSHIPS

The foundation of Serbian relationships is the
family, and family members of the same
generation—brothers, sisters, cousins—will often
be best friends. Other friendships are similarly
intimate and equally important. Relationships
developed in schools, colleges, local sports teams,
and workplaces tend to develop into lifelong
friendships.

The depth and openness of these relationships
means that friends offer support and help in all
matters—emotional, intellectual, or financial. An

individual's friend will be regarded and accepted as a friend of the whole family. Sayings such as "your friends are our friends" are often heard, and a friend's friend is immediately accepted into the wider circle of acquaintances. In this sense, social relations are more diverse and less atomized than in the West.

Serbian friendships are regularly maintained, and attempting to preserve a close relationship by means of an occasional phone call would be considered insulting. It is common for friends and family to telephone each other regularly, often daily—even if there is nothing new to talk about. Equally, Serbs visit each other's homes regularly, and people often drop by unannounced, just to say hello.

Serbs are generally open and laid-back, and it is easy to meet people and make casual acquaintances. Making true friends, however, naturally takes some time and perhaps the sharing of a common experience; but the typical Serb takes an active interest in new acquaintances, including foreigners, and will try to make new friends at any opportunity.

FORMS OF ADDRESS

In Serbia there are two different forms of address, formal and informal. When addressing a person in an informal way, "you" would be *ti* (the singular form), while the formal version would be *vi* (the plural form). People always address each other formally until the senior person, in age or relationship (for example, a manager), suggests otherwise.

The formal mode of address is used in everyday life when speaking to family elders, friends' parents, or parents-in-law. It is also used when talking to strangers, for example when buying a bus ticket or talking to a shopkeeper. In the workplace, managers are always addressed in the formal manner; and although work colleagues should be approached with the formal address, people who work together often agree to address each other informally.

Common exceptions where the informal *ti* is used as the norm are with grandparents, aunts, and cousins. Children are always addressed informally, and in the student world informality is also the norm.

SOCIAL CUSTOMS

When meeting people in informal environments, common greetings used are *"Ciao,"* *"Zdravo"* (Good health), or *"Gde ste?"* (How are you?). In more formal settings, people will say *"Dobar dan"* (Good day) or *"Dobro vece"* (Good evening).

When meeting people for the first time it is polite to shake hands, make eye contact, and say your full name and surname followed by *"drago mi je"* (pleased to meet you). Young people introduce themselves by the first name only, also followed by *"drago mi je."*

Firm handshakes are almost obligatory when meeting casually or formally, in any situation. If you are seated, it is polite to stand up when greeting other people, particularly women and elderly people. Kissing is a widespread form of greeting among friends, both male and female. The Serbian custom is to kiss three times on alternating cheeks, or to kiss only once when meeting on a regular basis. Making and maintaining eye contact is very important in any greeting situation; lack of eye contact is often considered rude.

It is considered polite to wish good day to someone sitting next to you on a bus, as well as to chat to a person waiting with you in a public space such as a health center or park. People will easily start a conversation with strangers and talk about their personal situations—something that might appear overly forward to Westerners. Serbs readily ask new acquaintances direct and personal questions, for example concerning their personal life or size of their salary. Serbs like getting to know other people, and are curious about different cultures and situations. Likewise, they will offer such information about themselves without hesitation.

Smoking is very widespread in Serbia and you can find hardly any nonsmoking areas, even in places where it is prohibited by law. Asking a stranger for a cigarette on the street or in a restaurant is common, and it would be impolite to refuse if you have some on you. People will offer cigarettes as an act of courtesy, so smokers can feel free to take one without obligation. Of course, smoking is a great way to meet like-minded smokers!

When visiting a church or monastery both men and woman are expected to cover their shoulders and legs, and hats should be removed. Inside any religious institution people are expected to be modest and quiet and to refrain from laughing or making loud conversation. It is not always acceptable to take photographs, so permission should be sought.

When a group of people goes out to a bar or a restaurant, the bill is usually paid in rounds, or split roughly between everyone. If you are invited for dinner your host will often pay the whole bill. Likewise, if you have invited someone for a drink or a meal, you will be expected to pick up the tab. However, these rules are not set in stone, and customs are changing depending on the people involved, especially as Serbia opens up to the rest of the world.

MEETING PEOPLE

Serbia is a hospitable place, and Serbs are warm and caring people. Many of the younger generation speak English, making communication fairly easy. Locals will always be thrilled when a tourist takes an active interest in their culture, and this can often be enough of a conversation starter.

Serbian cities and towns have continental-style pedestrian areas filled with cafés and bars, where people meet to share coffee and have a chat. The agreeable climate favors a café culture and al fresco dining, which helps to turn public spaces into very social environments. People are often in the mood to chat and in cafés you can always ask to join another table and try to make conversation.

In a village or town, curious locals might approach you in the central square, or while drinking coffee in a local establishment. If language isn't a barrier and they consider you a genuine person, invitations to visit them in their homes commonly follow.

The best way to experience the real tradition and customs of the Serbian way of life is at family and celebratory gatherings, and accepting invitations to such events is a must when the situation arises.

INVITATIONS HOME

Serbs love meeting and visiting each other on a regular basis, and it is common to receive invitations to people's homes, even when you have only known them a short while.

When visiting someone's home it is customary to remove your shoes before entering. It is polite for visitors to bring a present. Small presents such as fruit, cookies, or cakes are ideal when invited for coffee, but flowers, chocolate, and a bottle of wine or spirits are standard gifts when invited for dinner. Small presents for the children of the house are always appreciated—chocolates will do the trick.

An invitation for a casual coffee can be for any

time of the day, but this generally means early morning or afternoon. Coffee visits are brief, and within half an hour your host will be planning to get back to his or her chores. During this visit, the host will serve black home-brewed coffee (*Turska* or *domaća kafa*), with water, juice, and maybe *rakija* as well. *Slatko*, a sweet fruit preserve to be eaten with a spoon and a sip of water, is also offered as an aperitif.

For a lunch or dinner invitation, the time will be specified, and it is almost expected that guests arrive a little late—by about ten minutes or so. Dinner invitations are most common among the younger generation living in the cities, where late meals are becoming the norm, as in much of southern Europe. In other parts of the country, lunch is considered the main meal of the day and dinner will be on the early side.

Lunch or dinner parties last longer, a couple of hours at least. *Slatko*, followed by coffee, juice, and *rakija* will be served before the meal. Your host will refill an empty glass without warning, so it is wise to

leave some drink at the bottom of the glass if you don't want any more. Serbian hosts often provide a great quantity of food and drink, which can seem overwhelming. Vegetarians might find themselves shortchanged, however, unless it is Lent. The meal, although not particularly formal, usually consists of several courses including a starter, soup, main course, and dessert.

The hospitality and generosity of a Serbian host does not end at the meal. After a visit, especially in rural areas, your hosts will often offer you presents of seasonal fruit from their orchard or flowers from their garden.

CONVERSATIONS

Serbs are talkative and expressive people. They use body language to help add meaning and emotion to a conversation; face, body, and particularly hands will be in dramatic motion during even the most casual chat. Speech is regularly passionate and loud. Sometimes, a conversation that sounds like a heated argument to an outsider might simply be an everyday discussion about the weather.

English is widely spoken as a foreign language, and tourists are not expected to speak any Serbian. The Serbs are aware that their language is rather challenging to learn and are delighted when a foreigner tries to speak a few polite words.

As in other countries, talking about football (soccer) is a trusty social lubricant. Serbs are passionate sports supporters, and Serbia has had international success in many fields, including tennis, basketball, and football. In addition, Serb sportsmen play for teams all around the world, and locals might already be aware of the international leagues where their kinsmen compete, making sports a great topic for conversation.

A large proportion of people in Serbia, especially

those living in the cities, are university graduates. Reading is widespread, making books, magazines, and newspapers another popular topic for discussion, evident in the number of bookstores and stands on every main street.

One of the favorite topics for discussion across the Balkans is politics, and you are likely to get involved in rather serious political or economic discussions over a casual coffee. It is unusual for Serbs to engage in conversation with strangers about the general state of welfare in the country, the health service, or poor working conditions. People like to share their views, especially when dissatisfied with the way things are run at the political level.

Some political topics, however, must be broached with caution. For example, many Serbs still feel uneasy about their Croatian neighbors. More than 200,000 Serbs were expelled from their homes in Croatia during the 1992 Croatian war, and many are still living in social institutions or basic subsidized apartments.

Kosovo is another sensitive issue for the Serbs, as it is largely considered to be the historical heart of Serbia. Many Serbs oppose the partition of Kosovo and feel solidarity with the more than 300,000 Serbs who fled their homes in Kosovo in the late 1990s and early 2000s.

Serbs generally hold a grudge against the Western media, and will always try to explain how they were inaccurately portrayed and demonized during the run-up to the recent wars. It would be wise to approach discussions about the recent Balkan wars carefully, as Serbs commonly have a different view of events from those reported by the press around the world.

This bitterness, however, never extends to the personal level, and one would not be made to feel bad for being a Croat or a Westerner. Indeed, in practice there is actually a general solidarity between people from the ex-Yugoslav republics, although one would not understand this from television or newspapers in the West.

chapter five

DAILY LIFE

HOUSING

Modern Serbian houses are solidly built of concrete
and brick, with a yard and a porch or veranda often
surrounding one or three sides of the building. A
large communal area for living and dining will
dominate the floor space, with smaller bedrooms
to the side. Houses are generally arranged as single-
floor self-contained apartments, with multiple-
story houses capable of housing several generations
under the same roof. Roofs are four-sided, with
curved terracotta tiles, and have tall apexes in
areas of high precipitation—especially in the
mountains—while shallower pitched roofs are
common in the valley areas.

Traditional Serbian houses were built from
natural materials such as earth, stone, wood, and

later brick. This type of
construction is more
expensive today than
modern concrete and
cement fabrication, and
consequently rarer.
Traditional houses were
built in harmony with
their environment—

oriented to receive the most light and in alignment with the direction of underground water.

Before deciding where to lay the foundations, people would leave flat stones at several places around their land. If the stone was dry after a few days the area was considered to lack the appropriate energy for a home; if it had bugs and earthworms attached, this was a place of life and therefore suitable for building a house.

Countless wars over the centuries have ruined much of traditional Serbian architecture. After the devastation of the Second World War, the Communists built public housing in the form of the high-rise apartment blocks that now dominate many industrial towns and cities. Likewise, rural homes are now built of concrete rather than natural materials found in the surroundings.

People living in rural areas mostly build their own homes. In certain suburbs one can often see eccentric-looking villas, built by returning migrant workers and designed to impress with their nouveau-riche style.

In urban areas, housing is a rising problem especially for young people, as house prices are vastly out of proportion to wages and mortgage finance is hard to come by. Therefore, children tend to live with their parents well into adulthood. Hundreds of thousands now live in small apartments in the suburbs—particularly those who moved from villages in search of work, or those left impoverished by the Balkan wars. Those lucky enough to live in large inner-city apartments probably owned the property before the wars, or were allocated apartments in Communist times.

THE SERBIAN HOME

Serbian homes reflect the closeness of family relationships, with several generations often living under the same roof. Homes are built with large families in mind and can have numerous extensions, including whole new floors added to existing structures to accommodate the growing family. In rural areas family members build houses next to each other, so neighbors are often relatives. In the cities lack of space and the high cost of land makes it harder for extended families to live close together in this manner.

In a Serbian household, the woman of the house takes great pride in keeping her home impeccably clean and presentable. Homes are typically decorated with carpets, embroidery, and needlework. It is common to find cheap furniture from the 1970s and 1980s, as people do not earn enough to replace it and the market for higher-quality alternatives is not developed.

Kitchens are often open-plan to the dining room, and are well equipped with both gas (in a cylinder) and electric cooking facilities, for maximum self-sufficiency. Bathrooms are always built to a high specification, designed as wet rooms and tiled from floor to ceiling; mixer taps and bidets are standard.

Private home heating in urban areas is organized through district heating systems; there are about fifty boiler plants in the country, managed and financed by local government. These are primarily fueled by natural gas; the heat is distributed to private apartments via a network of insulated pipes, developed during the early Communist period. Boiler plants in Belgrade were targeted by NATO bombing in 1999, which left many city dwellers living in cold apartments. As a result, many people improvised additional heating sources such as wood-burning stoves or thermoelectric heaters.

Rural households have their own heating arrangements, with the central part of each house reserved for a coal or wood stove. One stove would generally be used to heat several rooms on a single floor, warming the kitchen and living areas and leaving bedrooms and bathrooms cold. Electric heaters and central heating systems are becoming increasingly common.

THE DAILY ROUTINE

In Belgrade, the daily bus, train, and tram services start at 4:00 a.m., and the streets get busy from 7:00 a.m., with peak congestion times on the roads 8:00 to 10:00 a.m. and 4:00 to 6:00 p.m.

Public-sector and government offices, police stations, and educational institutions often open at 8:00 a.m. and close for the day at 3:00 or 4:00 p.m.. Lunch breaks are not strictly determined and are usually taken as smaller coffee breaks several times a day. Public-facing services, such as the legal authorization of documents, open mostly in the morning only, but opening times vary from one institution to another.

Private businesses work similar hours to their Western counterparts, from 9:00 a.m. to 6:00 p.m., without strictly determined breaks. Pharmacies and health centers are open from 8:00 a.m. to 8:00 p.m., while food stores open from 6:00 a.m. to 10:00 p.m.

The school day varies depending on the type of school, the area, and the age of the pupils. The core working hours for schools doing one shift per day are 8:00 a.m. to 2:00 p.m. However, in many areas schools are overcrowded and are forced to run two shifts, in the morning and afternoon, with two different sets of pupils and teachers. Such schools will run from 7:00 a.m. to 7:00 p.m.

SHOPPING

Most people shop daily in a convenience store or in the markets. All areas have small convenience stores selling basic foodstuffs and necessities, open from 6:00 a.m. to 8:00 or 10:00 p.m. Western-style supermarkets have recently found their way into Serbia, and offer a great variety of stock including imported foods and toiletry products from well-known Western brands. These are more expensive and patronized by the better-off.

Preprepared food and frozen meals are unknown to most people. Everything is cooked from scratch; food is always washed and prepped at home before cooking, and most homes have a pantry as well as a large freezer.

For eggs and fresh meat, most Serbs buy local produce found at markets, butchers, or other specialized local stores. Meat is always bought fresh, and often a whole animal is bought from a farm and cut and packaged for home freezing.

Fresh bread is bought daily. The Serbs love baked goods, and bakeries can be found on every main street across the country, many working round the clock. As well as fresh breads of all sizes and grains, bakeries offer many salty and sweet pastries, *bureks*, rolls, and croissants.

The *pijaca* (open market) is the most popular place for food shopping, offering fresh produce directly from the farm (Belgrade's best-known markets are Kalenić Pijaca and Bajloni Pijaca). Open markets open and close early; anyone arriving after 10:00 a.m. will see only half of what was on offer at the start around 6:00 a.m. These markets offer seasonal fruit, vegetables, and herbs of exceptional quality and value. Indeed, Serbs are quite spoiled by the quality of this fresh produce. The perfect-looking fruit and vegetables of the supermarkets are considered artificial and "plastic" in comparison, and are commonly looked down upon.

Although prices are already very competitive, bargaining at the market is still acceptable. However, most farmers work hard and take great pride in their produce, so they might accept a lower price only for larger quantities. A common bargaining phrase is *"Može jeftinije?"* (Can it be cheaper?).

Clothes and accessories are available from many independent stores, open markets, and street sellers, as well as the larger shopping malls in the cities. Such stores are open from 10:00 a.m. until 7:00 p.m., and are closed on Sundays and bank holidays. Big shopping centers often stay open until 10:00 p.m.

There are numerous "bargain" shops selling imported goods from China, sometimes of questionable quality. In Belgrade and Novi Sad, well-known Western main-street brands can be found, as well as expensive designer stores with price tags well beyond the average local salary. Serbia has its own range of clothing brands, with designer labels such as PS, the children's brand Todor, and cheaper ranges such as Exit offering quality at attractive prices.

CHILDREN

As might be expected from such a family-oriented society, the Serbs are loving and affectionate toward children. Pregnant women are treated with the utmost respect, and many believe it lucky to fulfill a pregnant woman's wishes (especially food cravings) instantly. For this reason, pregnant woman are often offered free fruit at the market, or drinks at the café.

Babies and toddlers are frequently carried around by their parents or relatives, and are flooded with hugs and kisses wherever they go. People on the street are extremely friendly toward children, and in parks and play areas they will often talk to or kiss a child without the parent's permission.

Parents are very protective of their children, making sure they are well fed and dressed. It is common to see babies in the heat of summer in hats and socks and covered with blankets—an attempt maybe to keep out the famous Serbian "draft."

Female relatives offer lots of postnatal help during the early baby days. Later on, they will commonly provide child care when required, a great chance to get closer to the children. Together with the parents, relatives will have a strong influence over the education and upbringing of the little ones.

Where relatives are not available, nannies are the preferred child care option. In terms of formal child care, both private and state-subsidized kindergartens are offered from the age of three; only a few state-owned nurseries cater to children below that age.

THE EDUCATION SYSTEM

Education is highly regarded: compulsory education starts at the age of six and continues until fourteen. During this time children attend *osnovna skola*, or elementary school, for eight years, divided into lower and higher grades. The lower grades are first to fourth, where students have one teacher for all subjects, excluding English. Here they learn language and literature, mathematics, arts and music, physical education, and nature studies. In the higher grades, fifth to eighth, children study additional subjects such as history, geography, science, and a second foreign language; here they have one teacher per subject. In socialist Yugoslavia, governments put a lot of money into the education system, and virtually all primary schools in the country are free.

After elementary school, children can attend the secondary school of their choice, corresponding to the American high school, locally called *srednja škola* (middle school). Although these schools are not obligatory, most children attend. Elementary school grading will determine whether a child is eligible to apply, and entrance exam scores will determine who is entitled to a place. These schools are mostly state owned, but there are some private ones, especially in Belgrade, and both state and private schools follow the same national curriculum.

There are three types of high school in Serbia:
• Grammar schools, with courses lasting for four years. Students here study a broad range of subjects

and specialize in either the social sciences or the natural sciences.

- Professional schools, also with courses lasting four years. These offer a broad education, but students can specialize in a particular subject such as languages, mathematics, or science.
- Vocational schools, with courses lasting three years and specializing in a narrow discipline, such as cooking or plumbing. They do not give the option of continuing to university at the end of the course.

Higher education institutions include universities, art academies, and colleges, with courses lasting from three to six years. Acceptance to these institutions is based on secondary school grades and entrance exams. Postgraduate education is offered at several institutions, the most prestigious of which are based in Belgrade or Novi Sad.

While university education is often unaffordable for children from rural areas, many well-to-do Serbs send their children to Italian or British universities. Government grants are offered to many of the best students to attend state-owned faculties. For everyone else, private or state university fees are similar, with some specialized subjects such as medicine, dentistry, or architecture taking longer to complete and having significantly higher fees.

EMPLOYMENT

In 2012 Serbia reported a high rate of unemployment —around 20 percent. Almost half the unemployed are university graduates, large numbers of whom are former employees of the government or the public sector. The pressure of the economic crises and the advancing privatization programs have left many people jobless and with no income.

Low salaries combined with the high cost of living in the new market economy have led to general disillusionment among younger people, who account for a quarter of the unemployed. The employment market also suffers from a lack of clear regulations protecting workers' rights, working hours, and minimum wages, adding further to the gloomy outlook.

Those without university education commonly work in the service industries. The most widely available jobs for graduates are in administration, accounting, marketing, and trade. By contrast, the hardest jobs to find are for people trained in architecture, human resources, psychology, and sociology.

The most desirable jobs in Serbia are with big international corporations and well established public-sector businesses. These companies offer secure salaries, fixed working hours, guaranteed vacations, and sick leave. Many private-sector companies offer good salaries but demand longer working hours. Often they fail to pay their employees in a timely manner, and in these situations there is very little legal protection for the employee: a worker who ceases to work may lose all entitlement to unpaid wages, and so workers might be compelled to work for weeks or months without salary while the company sorts out its cash flow.

CONSCRIPTION

Until the law changed in 2011, all men under the age of thirty-five were required to complete twelve-months' military service. This was usually done after secondary school (at the age eighteen) or after finishing university. The only exemption from the draft was on medical grounds.

From January 1, 2011, military service ceased to be obligatory. However, one year's service is still compulsory for men or women wishing to work for the national army, security forces, or police. Most men living in Serbia in their thirties or above have served in the army, and many have seen conflict. This experience casts a long shadow on Serbian society, but also forms a strong bond of comradeship between those who have served.

SMOKING

Serbs are big smokers. Private get-togethers are often submerged in a thick cloud of cigarette smoke, and people regularly smoke in their homes even when small children are present. Cigarettes in Serbia are very cheap and can be bought in the supermarket, at all street kiosks, and at corner shops. The health consequences of smoking are not yet a big concern for the average Serb. Workplaces are nonsmoking, as are public gatherings held in closed spaces, such as concerts and cinemas. It is often hard to find nonsmoking areas in bars or cafés, while restaurants might offer a smoke-free zone right next to the smoking area.

TIME OUT

Serbian people today work longer hours and have less free time than their parents did. A couple of decades ago, people enjoyed a healthier work–life balance, often finishing their jobs by 3:00 p.m. However, even in today's hardworking environment, Serbs always make time to go out and socialize.

People use their leisure time to visit family and friends, go on excursions, and enjoy sports. Enormously sociable, they love doing things in big groups. They also take great pleasure in eating together, so many social events center around picnics, barbecues, and dinner parties at home or in restaurants.

SERBIAN CUISINE
Serbia's cuisine is rich and varied, and people are passionate about food. Serbian cooking is mostly influenced by Mediterranean—especially Greek and Turkish—and by Hungarian cuisine. Lunch is the main meal of the day. The portions are generous, and a starter in a Serbian restaurant might easily pass for a main course in another country.

Vegetarians in Serbia generally have a hard time, as most dishes contain meat. The diet is high in animal protein and vegetarianism is a little-known concept. If you are looking for vegetarian foods, it's best to ask for *posno jelo* (Lent dishes), as most Serbs observe the Lenten fast, which is the one way they can relate to not eating meat.

Serb Specialties

Typical Serbian foods include *slatko* (sweet preserves), *proja* (corn and polenta breads), *kajmak* (a young, soft cheese), *ajvar* (roast pepper and eggplant relish), *sarma* (pickled cabbage stuffed with  minced meat), beef prosciutto, and grilled meats. There are regional specialties, such as the spit-roasted pork of Šumadija, the spit-roasted lamb of Zlatibor, lamb cooked in milk from eastern Serbia, or grilled delicacies from Leskovac in the south.

Social and celebratory meals start with a toast of *rakija*; one must clink glasses while keeping direct eye contact and loudly proclaiming *"Živeli!"* (Cheers!). Typical first-course dishes include *kajmak*, *proja*, *ajvar* and cured meats, roasted peppers stuffed with cheese, or crisp-fried zucchini and eggplant served with soft cheese.

Salads are eaten as a side to the main dish, but also with the starters. In the past, different types of salad were served depending on the season: pickled cabbage or vegetables in winter and fresh salads in summer. Today this is still the case in rural areas, but a variety of salads is available all year round.

Supe (soups) and *čorbe* (broths) are often served at lunch. *Čorbe* are hearty broths full of meat and vegetables, while *supe* have the meat and vegetables

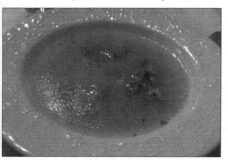

removed before serving and replaced with noodles. Stews and casseroles are also popular, especially the traditional *pasulj* (Serbian bean stew) consisting of white or brown beans prepared as a broth and served with pancetta, sausages, or pork chops.

Main courses revolve around grilled or roast meats such as *pljeskavice* (beefburgers), *uštipci*

(meatballs stuffed with cheese and smoked ham), *kobasice* (sausages), *krmenadle* (pork chops), *ražnjići* (shish kebab), and *vešalica* (strips of grilled smoked meat). *Ćevapčići* is one of the best-known grilled meats, prepared from minced beef rolled into finger-sized pieces and usually served in portions of ten with homemade flatbread. *Pečenje na ražnju*, or spit-roasted meats, are an integral part of Serbian cuisine, and no celebration can be without them. Many restaurants across the country have a rotating spit roast out front, with roast lamb or pork sold by the kilogram freshly carved from the spit.

Fish in Serbia usually comes from local rivers: carp, perch, catfish, or trout are most commonly served. Traditionally, fish is prepared in a number of different ways—for example, in a rich onion and tomato sauce, panfried and served with boiled potatoes and greens, or stuffed with smoked meats. *Riblja čorba* (fish broth) is extremely popular and when combined with bread is often a meal in itself. It is typically prepared from several types of high-quality white fish and served piping hot and spicy.

Traditional desserts include rich baklavas, walnut pie (baked puff pastry with ground walnuts and sugar paste), or small, dry, walnut-rich cakes called *orasnice*, baked in horseshoe shapes. Alternatively, a variety of fruit strudels is served, with fillings such as apple, cherry, or poppy seeds. Rich Viennese-style tortes with fruit or chocolate are also popular.

Serbs always finish their meals with coffee, commonly *domaća kafa* or espresso. *Domaća kafa* (home-brewed coffee) is also referred to as *crna kafa* (black coffee), Serbian coffee, or Turkish coffee. This is a strong coffee, prepared by boiling finely powdered roast coffee in a pot, with sugar added to taste. The coffee is then served in small cups and should be left for a few minutes before drinking to allow the sediment to settle at the bottom.

EATING OUT

Restaurants can be found everywhere in Serbia. Most serve inexpensive local foods, or Italian-style pastas and pizzas. Bakeries, sandwich bars, and fast-food shops selling grilled or barbecued food are also common and are great places to pick up good, inexpensive food. There is as yet no culture of corporate-style fast food as seen in the West.

A variety of restaurants and fine dining options is available in Belgrade or Novi Sad. In Belgrade, Chinese, Japanese, Mexican, and French cuisine are just some of the international options on offer. Often, however, this food will be prepared by Serbian chefs doing their "take" on a foreign style— leading to some interesting culinary combinations!

Live music is common in Serbian restaurants, with musicians playing old favorites in a designated area, as well as roaming from table to table. Those requesting a specific song are expected to tip the band.

TIPPING

Tipping is almost obligatory in cafés, bars, and restaurants, assuming the service has been satisfactory. A service charge is never included in the bill, and a tip of 10 percent is normal. Waiting staff will sometimes ask for a section of the bill to be settled if they are finishing their shift. It is also perfectly acceptable to pay the bill at the cash register if you're in a rush to leave.

In high-end places, the waiters' job is highly regarded and well paid. Such waiters are well connected and have plenty of local knowledge and noteworthy stories, so people often put a tip directly into their hands, followed by a firm handshake. This is also an excellent way of obtaining a table next time if the restaurant looks full.

Taxis are reasonably priced and, although a tip is not required, fares are often rounded up for ease of transaction. Likewise, in shops and markets no tipping is expected, but a small rounding of the total bill is common. Nobody expects to give or receive one dinar in change.

Dining establishments in Belgrade are concentrated in three main areas, although restaurants are scattered across the city. There are restaurants on rafts along the Danube on the Zemun side, where you can find the best *riblja čorba* in town. Around the fortress of Kalemegdan at the confluence of the Sava and Danube Rivers are many fine restaurants. The old town area of Dorćol is filled with popular bars and eateries, and contains the Skadarlija quarter—the old, cobbled, bohemian part of the city—filled with traditional Serbian restaurants where dining is accompanied by live music.

When visiting a restaurant in Serbia it is not necessary to book a table, and dress codes are mostly casual and relaxed. If a table is not marked "reserved," you may occupy it without waiting to be seated. Signaling waiting staff with the hand is perfectly normal, and waiters often respond with a curt "yes?". This is not considered impolite—just the Serbian manner, and totally reasonable.

SHOPPING FOR PLEASURE
Shopping for pleasure can be experienced in Belgrade and Novi Sad. The famous pedestrianized Knez Mihajlova street in the capital offers the best choice of main-street brands, while the streets around the old town quarter have exclusive boutiques. Shopping malls in both cities carry an extensive range of world brands. Small souvenir shops can be found at most tourist attractions, and local handicrafts can be bought along the promenades of historic sites such as Kalemegdan Fortress.

NIGHTLIFE
Nightlife is centered around the big cities. In Belgrade, an active nightlife can be enjoyed every

night of the week. People start their evenings in trendy cafés, bars, or restaurants, where entry is usually free, and which stay open until around 1:00 a.m. Those wanting to continue the evening head to a nightclub. Nightclubs don't start to fill up before midnight, and generally close at 4:00 a.m.— although some venues stay open all night.

Many nightclubs in Belgrade are located on floating rafts along the Danube and Sava riverbank, or around the walls of Kalemegdan Fortress. These are stylish places, serving elaborate cocktails in lavishly designed settings. The music on offer includes house, hip-hop, R&B, techno, and drum'n'bass, played by well-known local or European DJs. Also played in clubs and bars is the extremely popular Serbian musical subgenre of *turbofolk*, a cross between folk and dance music.

Belgrade is a bohemian city and home to many artists, so there is also a burgeoning underground nightlife scene. Impromptu all-night warehouse parties are held in abandoned Communist-era buildings, with artists' studios and "unofficial" bars also offering entertainment for the night.

Serbs don't need a particular reason for going out, whatever their age, lifestyle, or budget, although the older generations tend to prefer private parties in a restaurant, for example, rather than a nightclub. Even during the dark days of the UN embargo, with inflation rocketing and widespread poverty, bars and clubs were thriving, full of people eager to socialize and spend their last money on a round of drinks.

Indeed, Belgrade today is the "Balkan place to be," a nightlife hub drawing the youth from around the

region and beyond. Croatians, Bosnians, and
Slovenians often prefer Belgrade nightlife to their
own.

THE MUSIC SCENE

Serbia has a rich tradition of music, encompassing a
variety of instruments including bagpipes, flutes,
horns, lutes, and trumpets. Serbian folk music is
divided into rural and urban, with rural music
producing the famous two-beat sound played most
often on an accordion, to which people make a circle
and dance the *kolo*.

Urban folk, on the other hand, is performed with
violins and clarinets, often accompanied by simple
lyrics exploring famous loves and tragedies. The
subsequent modernization of this sound has
produced the best-selling genre of *novokomponovana
muzika*, or newly composed music.

Serbia has nurtured vibrant music scenes in other
genres, from the rock-based Yugoslav New Wave of

the 1980s to the current hip-hop scene, the modern jazz scene, and many quirky musical subcultures besides.

The brass band is probably the most recognizable manifestation of Serbian folk music. It was popularized by the indigenous Roma and is prominent in all major events in traditional Serbian life—births, deaths, baptisms, weddings, and farewell parties. The brass band forms the quintessential "Balkan sound," and it is no wonder Serbia hosts the famous Guča festival every year, the largest trumpet or brass-band festival in the world. The Guča festival sees hundreds of thousands of people attending this wild and chaotic event, which started life as a casual assembly of trumpet players in the small town of Guča in central Serbia. This festival is indicative of the quality, energy, and craziness of traditional Serbian folk culture.

Classical music lovers can find several philharmonic orchestras performing in concert halls around the country. There are numerous classical music festivals in Serbia, including international cello, harp, and piano festivals. Serbia has produced some famous composers, the best-known being Stevan Stojanović Mokranjac.

FILM AND THEATER

Serbia has a mature and robust film industry that continuously produces internationally acclaimed films, actors, and filmmakers including the famous Emir Kusturica, one of the few directors to have won two Palmes d'Or at the Cannes Film Festival. The industry reached its peak in the 1980s, and still continues to service domestic and international productions, including the odd Hollywood movie. There are nearly two hundred cinemas across the country, showing both local and international films.

Serbia has a rich theatrical tradition, embracing everything from fringe productions to bigger-budget crowd-pleasers. The National Theater, founded in the mid-nineteenth century, is the oldest theater company in Serbia. Along with its many theater productions, it stages opera and has an established ballet company.

FESTIVALS

There are plenty of annual cultural events and festivals across the country, dedicated to every aspect of the arts or to culinary accomplishments. Prominent cultural festivals in Belgrade include FEST, the International Film Festival, which regularly

attracts film stars from the West; BELEF, the
Belgrade summer festival, with performing arts,
visual arts, and music; BITEF, the International
Theater Festival; and the International Belgrade
Book Fair.

Just north of Novi Sad, the small village of Turija
is famous for the Kobasicijada, a sausage festival that
attracts tens of thousands every year. And in recent
times, Novi Sad has become known internationally
for the famous "Exit," a popular music festival held
there every summer in the grounds of the
breathtaking Petrovaradin fortress, bringing an
influx of European tourists and trade.

Festivals in western Serbia include the Drina
Regatta, when thousands float down the river on
wooden rafts; Pršutijada, a festival in the village of
Mačkat dedicated to smoked ham; and the
International Fine Art Colony of Ceramics held near
Užice, which attracts artisans from around the world.

Every year, the main boulevard of the southern Serbian town of Leskovac is closed for a weeklong festival called Roštiljijada, where food stalls are erected in the street and food-themed competitions are held— for example, a competition to create the biggest hamburger. On the cultural side, the southern town of Niš hosts the Nišville Jazz Festival, the Choral Festival, and the Festival of Actors' Achievements, among others.

SPORTS

The Serbs are extremely keen sportspeople, excelling in a variety of fields, as is evident in the hundreds of sports facilities and stadiums across the country. The country's socialist heritage and agreeable climate are both partly responsible for the popularity of amateur team sports. Local five-a-side football pitches are booked up well in advance, late into the night on weekdays and weekends alike. Basketball courts are regularly filled with young people and if not used for basketball are often turned into improvised tennis courts.

Serbs are equally ardent supporters and fans. European and world leagues are keenly followed because of the success of Serb players performing internationally. None is more popular than the English Football Premiership. One notable success in this league is Nemanja Vidić, made Manchester United captain in 2011.

In the local football league, one of the greatest rivalries in the country is between Red Star and

Partizan, both from Belgrade. This rivalry has been ongoing since the Second World War, and is often supported by anarchic and passionate displays from the stands, which sometimes result in violence. Red Star Belgrade won the European Cup Championship and Intercontinental Cup Championship in 1991, after which Serbian sportsmen were banned from competing internationally for most of the decade under the UN Embargo.

The Serbs punch above their weight in international sporting competitions, and Belgrade has hosted major events including the European basketball and volleyball championships and the Davis Cup for tennis. Tennis has only recently become accessible in Serbia and is now one of the most popular sports in the country. This is partly thanks to the winning Davis Cup national team of 2010, and to Novak Djoković's success at the Grand Slam tournaments, becoming the world number one in 2011.

Serbs are also great lovers of basketball. The Serbian player Vlade Divac played alongside Magic Johnson in his early career and later became an NBA All-Star and a well-known face across the US media.

HEALTH TOURISM

Serbia is blessed with many hot and cold mineral springs, natural mineral gases, and medicinal mud. Many of these are used for health tourism in spa resorts, or *banja*. These resorts are popular with people who wish to spend time in areas of great natural beauty, in rolling hills or gentle valleys surrounded by forests, meadows, and orchards.

The Serbs are keen spa-goers, and many will spend at least one week of their annual leave on a visit. Business groups commonly use the facilities for team-building exercises and seminars. School excursions visit for physical training sessions, as do national and professional sports teams and athletes preparing for big games.

Banjas are mostly favored by the elderly and by people recovering from illness. They offer wellness programs and spa therapies that involve drinking medicinal water and taking medicinal mud baths, combined with a physical exercise program. Most have fitness centers and sports fields, and promise to restore physical and spiritual vitality over a week. There are over forty spas in Serbia, the most visited being Banja Koviljača, Vrnjačka Banja, Sokobanja, and Prolom Banja. Some of these are characterized as "climatic spas" because of their geographic location at altitudes of over 3,000 feet (1,000 m).

SOME "MUST-SEE" DESTINATIONS

Belgrade: Kalemegdan Fortress, Old Town and Skadarlija, the National Museum of Serbia, the Ethnographic Museum, the Nikola Tesla Museum, St. Mark's Church in Tašmajdan Park; the Temple of St. Sava.

Novi Sad: Petrovaradin fortress.

Western Serbia: Zlatibor Mountain, Mokra Gora national park, Drvengrad ethno-village.

Eastern Serbia: Đjerdap national park, Smederevo and Golubac fortresses, Lepenski Vir Mesolithic settlement, the Roman ruin of Felix Romuliana.

Southern Serbia: Đavolja Varoš on the Radan Mountain, the Skull Tower in Niš, Crveni Krst concentration camp in Niš.

TRAVELING

Serbia has a very good transportation infrastructure. The road network is well maintained and driving around the country is a pleasure.

GETTING THERE

Serbia is well positioned in southern Europe, easily accessible by road from Vienna, Budapest, Prague, Thessaloniki, or Sofia. One day's driving will get you to Milan or Frankfurt, making Serbia an easy destination for people living in central Europe.

If driving a private car into Serbia, drivers will need a European or international driver's license, the vehicle's registration / ownership documents, and green card insurance. Serbia is generally not covered in standard pan-European insurance policies. Insurance can normally be purchased at the border, costing around €80 / US $100 / £60 per month.

Established bus routes link Serbia with all the surrounding countries, and travelers can get to Belgrade by bus from as far afield as London, Paris, or Malmö. Lasta is the Serbian Eurolines partner, and they have the best buses in the country.

Flights to Belgrade depart from most European centers. Notable budget carriers include Wizz Air, Germanwings, Norwegian Air, Flyniki, SpanAir, and airBaltic. Jat Airways is the national carrier, based at Belgrade's Nikola Tesla Airport and flying to forty destinations worldwide. Serbia has three international airports: Belgrade, Niš, and Vršac.

It is possible to use the European rail network to travel to Serbia: trains to Novi Sad, Niš, and Belgrade depart from Prague (15 hours to Belgrade), Vienna (10.5 hours), and Budapest (7.5 hours). There are direct trains running between Belgrade and Zurich, Munich, Ljubljana, Sofia, Bucharest, and Bar. Reservations may be required, especially during holiday periods.

Greek Railways suspended its international trains in 2011, so travel on the Thessaloniki–Belgrade route should be confirmed close to the travel date.

ARRIVING IN SERBIA

Citizens of EU countries, the Swiss Confederation, Norway, Iceland, and the USA may enter Serbia using passports, and visas are granted on arrival for up to ninety days. EU citizens and citizens of the former Yugoslav republics may enter with valid ID cards, but it is still safer to bring a passport. Other nationals will need to arrange a short-stay visa beforehand, issued by a Serbian embassy or consular service.

Foreigners are required to register with the local police within twenty-four hours of arrival. If they are staying in a hotel this will be done by the reception staff on checking in. Although many visitors choose not to register, they risk a fine or detention at the border when attempting to leave the country.

A longer stay requires a temporary residence permit, which can be obtained in-country from the same police authority with whom you are registered. To avoid any misunderstanding at the border, it is important to ensure both entry and exit stamps are correctly stamped into your passport, as this can sometimes be overlooked on smaller, more remote border crossings.

Special care should be taken when crossing from Kosovo to Serbia, as the Serbian government does not accept the authority of the Kosovan government, borders, or immigration officers. Therefore entry points from Kosovo, or those on Kosovo's external borders, are not recognized. Do not attempt to enter Serbia for the first time from Kosovo. Only enter Serbia from Kosovo if you have already traveled into Kosovo via Serbia.

It is a legal requirement always to carry identification (passport, ID card) on your person, and Serbian police may stop you and request this documentation at any time.

TRAVELING AROUND

As would be expected from a formerly socialist country, the public transportation infrastructure is highly developed and relatively inexpensive. An extensive rail network connects the whole country. However, trains are generally slower than buses as a result of lack of investment over the last forty years, and the rolling stock is often of poor quality. The advantage of train travel is that journeys are extremely scenic and often very sociable.

The bus and coach network is similarly extensive, with a variety of different players in the market. Local buses are generally of poor quality, but intercity coaches are of European standard. Buses are reliable and generally leave on time, although arrival times can vary depending on the traffic, the state of the roads, and any border crossings along the way.

Outside the cities, minor roads in Serbia are not always well maintained. Unlike the major expressways connecting the large cities, in rural areas the road is sometimes reduced to a single-lane, winding dirt track. Therefore, expect slow progress with variable road conditions. It is not uncommon to be stuck behind a horse-drawn cart laden with agricultural or industrial materials.

Road signs could do with a lot of improvement, so if you are traveling independently on the roads be sure to take an up-to-date map. Car drivers must carry with them all their documents, including passport, driver's license, registration, and insurance certificate, plus certain compulsory equipment as per European norms. The police can and do stop vehicles to check for this equipment, and have the ability to fine you for noncompliance. The police also regularly check for speeding using a radar gun, and if an oncoming vehicle flashes its headlights at you it probably means there is a police speed check ahead of you—the other driver is trying to warn you.

DRIVING IN SERBIA

Compulsory Equipment: Hazard warning triangle, spare bulb set, first aid kit, at least 10 ft (3 m) of towing rope, spare tire, reflective jacket (kept in the passenger compartment of the vehicle, not the trunk).

Insurance: Third party insurance is obligatory. Green card insurance is recognized if marked with the letters SRB.

In the Winter (November 1–April 1): winter tires are obligatory. Snow chains must also be carried at all times.

Speed Limits: 30 mph (50 kmph) in towns, 50 mph (80 kmph) on undivided highways, 60 mph (100 kmph) on divided highways, and 75 mph (120 kmph) on expressways.

Tolls: All expressways have tolls. Tolls range from €2.00 to €20.00 / US $3.00 to US $30.00 / £1.50 to £15.00 depending on the size of the vehicle, and it is advisable to carry cash for payment (dinars preferred, but euros accepted).

Headlights: It is obligatory to use daytime lights or low-beam headlights during the day.

Driving Offenses: Police officers will issue a ticket. Foreigners are not allowed to pay fines on the spot, but must settle a ticket at a post office. Serious offenses have to be dealt with in court.

Seat Belts: Use of front and rear seat belts (where they are installed) is compulsory.

Passengers/Children: Persons under the influence of alcohol and children up to the age of twelve are not permitted to travel as front-seat passengers. Children under the age of three may travel in the front seat in a rear-facing child seat with the airbag deactivated.

Alcohol: The alcohol level in the bloodstream may not exceed 0.03 percent (approximately one drink). For motorcyclists, novice drivers, and professional drivers this value is 0 percent. Police carry out random breath alcohol tests, and always test after an accident. Those refusing a test will be automatically imprisoned.

Motorcycles: Helmets are obligatory for driver and passenger. Passengers must not be under the influence of alcohol. Children under the age of twelve are not permitted as passengers.

Car Rental: If renting a car in another Balkan state such as Croatia or Bosnia, you cannot automatically drive to Serbia (or vice versa) without having first arranged this with the vehicle rental firm. Insurance is not automatically transferred between states. Many Serbian car rental firms do not allow their vehicles to be driven in Kosovo, Albania, or Bulgaria.

GETTING AROUND BELGRADE

Belgrade has an extensive public transportation system consisting of buses, trams, trolleybuses, and trains. The vehicles are often basic, but the network reliably connects all parts of the city, including the outlying suburbs. During rush hour, public transportation is always crowded.

Prices are cheap (RSD50 / €0.50 / US $0.80 / £0.30 from a kiosk, or RSD100 / €1.50 / US $1.30 / £0.70 from the driver) and tickets must be validated on the vehicle in manually operated punching machines.

Transportation authorities routinely check tickets for validation, especially at rush hour, and a fine is around €30.00 / US $40.00 / £25.00. If you are staying for an extended period, it is worth purchasing a pass that lasts from two to four weeks. This can be done only at the local public transportation office.

There are around 120 urban and 300 suburban bus lines, and the bus fleet is mostly modern. Bus transportation runs twenty-four hours a day; night buses run between midnight and 4:00 a.m. and are less frequent, running approximately every half hour to every hour.

There are twelve tramlines and eight trolleybus lines in Belgrade, three of which connect to New Belgrade. The trams are mostly old and creaking, but this is a very atmospheric and efficient way to travel. Trams run very frequently between 4:00 p.m. and midnight. Of particular interest is the scenic tramline 2, which travels on a circular route around the city center in both directions. Trams and trolleybuses run only in Central Belgrade; for outlying areas you must take an ordinary bus.

There are nine public and many more private minibus lines, which are smaller and quicker than regular buses, and also more expensive. The routes

are slightly obscure, in that most stops do not show minibus routes and one must wait for the bus to show up to discover the route (or research the information beforehand). Seven train lines connect

Belgrade's outer suburbs to the city; however, these trains are generally unreliable and often late. Two underground stations in downtown Belgrade (Vukov Spomenik and Karađorđev Park) are used by a couple of these train lines. There is no metro/subway system as yet in Belgrade.

Taxis are cheap and plentiful. You can hail a taxi on the street or order one by phone. When ordering by phone, a 15 percent discount on the fare is often applied. In town, taxis always run on the meter, although it is possible to agree to a fixed price if coming from the airport. It is usual to round up the fare. Taxis regulated by the city carry a little blue sticker with the city coat of arms and a number on it, and often have a registration plate ending with TX. Privately owned cabs (with an illuminated white sign on the roof) can be more expensive.

Finding a parking space in Belgrade is difficult because of the number of vehicles on the roads, and illegally parked cars are likely to be towed away. The restrictions are sometimes obscure, and rumor has it that the authorities prioritize towing away cars with foreign registration plates—so, even if you see other vehicles parked in a particular area, this does not mean you are safe. It will cost in the region of €100 /US $140 / £85 to free a vehicle from the car pound. Parking lots and metered parking are a safe bet, but be aware of maximum parking times, which are usually one, two, or three hours respectively in red, yellow, or green zones.

Private drivers should also be aware that Belgrade suffers enormously from congestion, especially during rush hours. Cars are not allowed to venture into yellow lanes, which are reserved for public transportation.

MONEY

The official currency of Serbia is the dinar (RSD), although euros are also accepted in some places. At the time of writing in 2012, common exchange rates were: £1.00 = RSD120, €1.00 = RSD103, US $1.00 = RSD77.

Credit cards and traveler's checks are accepted in many larger hotels and shops, and ATMs are very common in towns and cities, accepting international bank cards.

Currency exchange booths are common in the cities and at the airport. It is recommended to exchange currency through official exchange offices and banks, and not through illegal black-market street dealers.

If bringing more than €10,000 in cash into the country (or the equivalent in another currency), you are required to declare it on arrival.

HEALTH CARE

Serbia has a good public health care system free at the point of use, although many people still choose the convenience and quality of the private system.

Doctors and health care professionals are highly trained and competent, and most doctors will speak English, so you are in good hands. However, the quality of some equipment and standards of hygiene may not be up to Western standards.

Pharmacies supply many medicines and medical supplies, but tend not to stock the same brands that can be purchased in the West.

Comprehensive medical insurance is recommended for all travelers, as foreigners are charged for treatment. Hospitals and doctors usually require payment in cash or card for all services.

Serbia has a reciprocal health care agreement with many EU states, including the UK, providing treatment in genuine emergencies. For UK nationals, the documents needed for this emergency medical treatment are a UK passport, evidence of insurance in the UK, and evidence of registration with the local police.

Preventable Health Risks
Travelers to Serbia should be up to date with the recommended vaccinations, and for most people these will be adequate. The risks preventable by vaccine are hepatitis A, hepatitis B, and tetanus. Hepatitis A is transmitted through water, so boiled or bottled water only should be drunk, especially in Vojvodina, where the risk is slightly higher.

Rabies is a low risk, and unless you are traveling to remote areas where medical care is not readily available, it is probably not strictly necessary to take a pre-exposure vaccination.

Tick-borne encephalitis (TBE) is another low risk. It is a risk in areas around the city of Belgrade, with ticks most active during early spring to late autumn. Travelers who engage in outdoor activities in areas of vegetation are most at risk. There is a TBE vaccine, but it is probably enough to avoid ticks by means of insect repellent and protective clothing.

SAFETY

Recent wars, the tense situation regarding Kosovo, and isolated pockets of die-hard ultranationalism might lead one to believe that Serbia is a dangerous place. While it may be true that Serbia is a little "edgier" than some of its European neighbors, most visits to Serbia are trouble free and there is generally nothing to worry about, provided travelers are mindful of their surroundings.

It is advisable to avoid large crowds and demonstrations, especially passionate protests in Belgrade, for example regarding issues such as Kosovo or the Pride March for gay rights. Most protests pass without incident, but some have seen violence at the fringes. Wins or losses in sporting events can also trigger unrest.

Organized crime in Serbia is not directed against foreigners, and low-level street crime is much as in other parts of Europe. Commonsense rules apply: be vigilant in public places, and avoid flaunting valuable possessions.

While tensions continue along the Serbia–Kosovo border, it is best to avoid the area unless absolutely necessary. Remember, you may not travel from Kosovo to Serbia unless you began your journey in Serbia and are returning there.

Residual land mines and unexploded ordnance remain a problem in certain parts of the country. Previously affected woodland and agricultural land in the Croatia, Bosnia and Herzegovina, and Serbia tri-border area is now generally considered safe from land mines. At the time of writing, an investigation of reports about possible land mine areas on the borders between Kosovo and Serbia is under way.

Cluster-bomb contamination and unexploded aerial bombs and projectiles still pose a larger problem, affecting a significant number of locations across the country. Take care if traveling in these areas, and do not stray from roads and paths without an experienced guide. Such areas are marked with warning signs.

Health and safety laws are not well developed in Serbia; be aware of this when attending nightclubs, restaurants, theaters, or other public venues, as maximum occupancy and fire safety regulations may not be up to Western standards.

In remote, mountainous areas, wild animals such as boars, bears, and wolves still roam. If traveling to such areas, take the proper precautions and use an experienced guide.

Natural disasters, including earth tremors and forest fires, afflict certain parts of the country, particularly the uninhabited mountainous areas, although serious earthquakes are rare. Take care when visiting dry areas and make sure cigarette butts are properly disposed of, to prevent outbreaks of fire.

chapter eight

BUSINESS BRIEFING

Positioned on the doorstep of the EU, with a well-developed road, rail, and waterway infrastructure connecting Europe to Western Asia, Serbia enjoys a fantastic position for transcontinental trading, with easy access to 30 million regional consumers. In addition, it has preferential trading status with the USA, the EU, and the Russian Federation.

Serbia is a rapidly developing market for foreign investment, with political, economic, and social reforms creating great growth potential. In 2006, Serbia was ranked by the World Bank as the number one business reformer in the world, with approximately US $14 billion in foreign currency reserves, and an export market valued at US $9 billion (in 2007), exporting mostly to Italy, Germany, and Russia.

The highest-ranking businesses in Serbia are fuel traders (particularly oil companies), followed by the electricity companies, which are still not fully privatized. In addition, a number of multinational retailers, telecommunications firms, and several ex-socialist metallurgical producers can be added to the list of top businesses.

The most profitable sector in Serbia in 2010 was building materials production, with net profit margins of almost 30 percent. The biggest growth was reported by the chemical industry (88 percent) and the metal industry (70 percent).

On the downside, Serbia inherited almost a quarter of the former Yugoslavia's debt; external debt (approximately half public, half private) in 2010 was US $30 billion. Many areas of the economy, such as iron production, textiles, and IT development, are seriously neglected. Wars and economic sanctions have caused much of the economy to lag behind current Western standards. However, Serbia has a highly skilled labor force and an entrepreneurial class eager for new challenges. The Serbs are eager to adopt EU business practices and to meet the standards of Western consumers, making Serbia an attractive investment opportunity.

BACKGROUND

From the 1950s to the early 1980s, the planned economy of the Communist Party in former Yugoslavia created substantial economic growth. The period was marked by an impressive industrialization effort, with improved infrastructure, engineering technology, and efficiency. However, in the 1990s, conflict forced many state companies out of business. Some could no longer continue production because parts were made in different constituent republics involved in war, while others lost access to their markets.

The economic sanctions imposed by the international community had a devastating effect. Inflation rocketed, destroying the economy and clearing out the state's foreign reserves. With shops regularly empty, citizens were forced to purchase goods on the black market, fueling an unregulated underground economy. By the Bulldozer Revolution of October 2001, many Serbian industries were worthless.

After the fall of Yugoslavia, Serbia moved from a command economy to a Western-style free-market economy, but in such a way that privatization was carried out before denationalization was completed. Many believe that this process contributed to social upheaval, with no adequate safeguards in place to protect the collective wealth. Companies or individuals that responded in time secured their positions as regional players. The purchase of state-developed enterprises at reduced rates proved highly profitable to a well-placed few, facilitating market dominance for certain companies (especially supermarket chains, banks, and oil companies) or encouraging asset stripping and other nonproductive activity. Much of the remaining industry was subsequently sold to foreign investors.

Although they were officially conducted through tenders, some of these transactions are still highly disputed, and certain individuals involved in the tendering processes are sought by the Serbian authorities or Interpol. For most of the population, however, privatization and denationalization meant almost immediate unemployment and a future with little or no security.

PEOPLE IN POWER

Serbia has experienced only a short period of parliamentary democracy. Many political and economic changes are ongoing, with old structures constantly being removed while new practices are imposed. Present-day Serbia is still a crude version of a developed state, with much room for improvement.

The fall of Communism saw many of the Communist old guard reposition themselves in respected jobs in academia or in other honorary roles. However, many still hold power, ironically as newborn capitalists. Many people in these positions were former Party members, or have relatives who held high ranks in the Party, and they are still respected for their former affiliations by the working classes, where the Communist values of justice and equality persist.

Many of the current power magnates are businesspeople who made their fortunes during the war years. Some were affiliated with Slobodan Milošević's Socialist Party of Serbia, others with the G17 Plus, a US-funded NGO (and later political party) made up of economists specializing in privatization. Many individuals also became extremely wealthy during this period by providing on the black market basic goods and services no longer available because of the economic sanctions, for example cigarettes, gasoline, medicine, and foreign currency.

Serbian yuppies work mostly in foreign companies and banks, or run their own businesses. They enjoy a standard of living closer to the Western norm, and can be seen throughout the major cities doing what all yuppies do: looking busy, using English buzzwords, talking about their foreign vacations, communicating on the latest Apple gadgets, and treating anything local with disdain.

BUSINESS CULTURE

In the new Serbian capitalism there is little or no job security, and workers' rights are limited. In the private sector, employees are often too afraid of losing their positions to permit inefficiency and coffee drinking during working hours. Many are infatuated with the Western model, and feel that hard work, long hours, competence, and efficiency are the natural order.

Public-sector businesses continue to work at a much slower pace. They have inherited many of the old practices regarding working hours, and have a much healthier work–life balance. As anywhere else, big public institutions are slow to improve and adapt to new markets and management styles.

In post-Communist countries, there is a history of decision making by committee, or communal management styles where groups met together to create plans. However, these plans were seldom implemented, leading to apathy and cynicism among workers. Therefore, in Serbia the older generation lacks the drive and energy of its younger counterpart.

In some municipalities, considerable effort has been made to improve efficiency, cut waiting times, and simplify bureaucracy by adopting modern business models. This type of reform, although rare, has improved the business climate, attracting new business and inspiring existing concerns to do the same. For example, efforts by the mayor of Belgrade have improved the quality of public services across the capital, although they still vary between councils within the city.

Stereotypical examples of the public-sector worker can still be found—the public employee drinking coffee and having a casual chat with a colleague, while approximately seventy-five people jockey for position in front of the single open counter. Even the simple matter of picking up one's newly issued passport can last for days, with camping in line almost mandatory.

The Serbian labor market, however, is turning its back on old Communist conventions and is slowly adopting modern practices. This is particularly obvious in the service industry, as business models developed in the EU are fast becoming the norm for both employer and employee.

Corruption

As mentioned, corruption is a problem in Serbia. The legal vacuum left by the collapse of Yugoslavia has encouraged high-level corruption, organized

crime, tax evasion, and other financial fraud, which have been exacerbated by an underdeveloped civil society. On the controversial Transparency International index of perceived corruption, Serbia features approximately halfway down the list of 183 countries.

Financial corruption is most likely to occur in public procurement, privatization, and areas with other large expenditures. It is also recognized that health care, political party funding, and the judiciary are areas of concern. Serbia has taken steps to rectify some of these problems, and ongoing reforms and initiatives, aimed at joining the EU, are returning many of these areas to some semblance of "normality." Previously, a contract was often considered an irrelevant piece of paper; and money, once it changed hands, could not easily be traced. In recent years, legislation has been enacted to protect foreign investors and to make the business climate more compliant.

PERSONAL CONTACTS

Personal relationships are the *modus operandi* in all spheres of Serbian life. This is a country where friends and family connections are vital, with business relations often shading unapologetically into nepotism. Serbs prefer to engage in business based on personal relationships or relationships created directly or via a third party. In a country where family is so important and ultracompetitive business practices have yet to take hold, it is no surprise that family and personal connections are favored in the work environment.

Nevertheless, the open channels of business function as they do anywhere else, with contact information available on relevant Internet sites. And, like anywhere in the world, being part of the "old boys' club," or knowing someone personally, will certainly help your cause.

PUNCTUALITY

Punctuality is a relative term everywhere in the Balkans—if it matters to you, then you are certain to be on time! In social situations, punctuality is considered to be almost rude, fifteen to thirty minutes late being regarded as on time.

When dealing with public-sector staff, punctuality is often an issue, simply because of inadequate staffing levels for that particular service. In the private sector, however, this type of slackness is almost unheard of.

Fortunately, these punctuality issues should not concern the foreign visitor, because by the time you experience your first belated appointment, your host will have won you over with great food, coffee, and a winning smile. Within a couple of visits to Serbia, your own sense of punctuality will cease to appear convincing and become somewhat unnatural. After all, you look as though you could definitely do with another espresso, and maybe a bite to eat, before you go into the details of whatever meeting you were going to have!

BUSINESS MEETINGS

An e-mail and/or a phone conversation will suffice to arrange a business meeting. In the absence of prior contact with the party in question, it is imperative to e-mail first, and follow up with a phone call to ensure the recipient has received the message. The venue will usually be by mutual agreement, and can vary from the office to a restaurant, café, or bar.

Shake hands with your counterparts, and be sure to look them directly in the eye when doing so. Maintain eye contact throughout the conversation—not doing so may be perceived as weakness or insincerity. The business dress code in Serbia is similar to that in Western countries—a suit and a tie, or trouser suit, will do fine. Overall, there are no particular formalities at business meetings, although everyone expects to be treated with respect.

Foreigners are warmly welcomed throughout the country, and it is the same in business dealings. Humor and joking by your host are a sign of comradeship, and should be taken as such. Your host's attempts to pamper you should be appreciated and gracefully accepted. It is vital to recognize that business etiquette varies from person to person, and company to company. The most important aspect of the exchange is what you bring to the table, because that will set the tone.

Be aware that both your proposal and your character will be judged. Personal likes and dislikes play an important part in the business conversation, arguably more so than the details of the deal in question. You are expected to sell yourself as well as your proposal, so don't forget to ask about the wife and kids, or inquire about recent sporting achievements.

PRESENTATIONS

The Serbs are quite businesslike and appreciate a straightforward approach, presenting all the salient points in a concise manner. On the other hand, everyone appreciates an imaginative, lively presentation laced with interesting detail and humor. The monotonous read-through of a

preprepared electronic presentation is a dead end—
few will listen, and most of the participants' energy
will be channeled into texting or anticipating the
coffee break. Even a small group of select
professionals will welcome an innovative
presentation. Allow time for a lengthy Q&A session,
as people will be keen to investigate further and to
"pick your brains."

NEGOTIATION
The Serbs are tough negotiators. The initial offer
you bring to the table should be reasonable, but
should leave room for maneuver. Expect to have
several meetings to hammer out the fine details
of any deal. Each item on the agenda will be
analyzed before it is agreed upon, and bureaucracy
and red tape are common, especially for deals in
the public sector.

It is not uncommon for Serbs to raise their voices
during business talks. However, this is not expected
of foreigners and it is advisable not to follow suit.
Raised voices are not considered "shouting," rather
a sign that issues are being discussed passionately.

Translating and Interpreting

Language specialists are easy to come by in Serbia, equipped with court-accredited bilingual and multilingual interpreting skills. The level of service is generally high, and while many interpreters are freelancers, most are employed by specialist firms. Rates vary, but €50 (US$66) per hour was the average in 2012 for accredited interpreters.

CONTRACTS

The courts in Serbia have been recently reformed and a new set of judges now presides. As a consequence, legal contracts are much more secure than in the past, the "wild west" image of Serbian business practices mostly consigned to history.

Major agreements and contracts—for example between commercial bodies—must be certified before they become legally binding. This certification is done by the local council or court, where the document will be stamped for a small administration fee. Smaller agreements and contracts can still be valid even if not certified in this way.

Lawyers in Serbia are affordable, and it is easy to find experts in their field—often with multilingual skills. It is not necessary to hire one when signing a contract, but advisable for a deal of any major value, or simply if you are not familiar with Serbian bureaucracy.

BUSINESS MEALS

Business meetings or negotiations often take place in the restaurant over lunch. Meals are never hurried when business is being discussed. Having enough time to eat is important, and no one will expect you to rush through a lunch—after all, it's bad for digestion.

Even purchasing a small plot of land from your neighbor might include a three-course meal or a small roast animal. Naturally, alcohol will also play an important role in the negotiations; returning to work tipsy, however, is frowned upon, and drunkenness is a big no-no.

BUSINESS GIFTS

In accordance with EU laws, the Serbian government has introduced measures to limit bribery, categorizing gifts that are legally acceptable in a business environment.

Nevertheless small gifts, such as convivial luncheons and presents from your country of origin, are the norm for any business transaction in Serbia, because they are also the norm in everyday life. Giving small gifts to business partners is a sign of consideration and affection, and shows respect. If you are visiting Serb colleagues from abroad, symbolic inexpensive presents will be appreciated, such as pens with a company logo, notebooks, key rings, or chocolates and cookies from your home country.

WOMEN IN BUSINESS
Woman have complete equality in Serbia and are found at every level of business life. Foreign businesswomen will find no problems at all when dealing with their Serbian counterparts.

chapter nine

COMMUNICATING

THE LANGUAGE

Serbian is a Southern Slavic language, originating in Old Church Slavonic and with a literary history dating back to the tenth century. The language was called Serbo-Croat (or Serbo-Croatian) during Yugoslav times. After the breakup of the country in the 1990s, the different national groups established their own variants of Serbo-Croatian as official languages—Serbian, Montenegrin, Croatian, and Bosnian—even though some of their own populations still referred to the mother tongue as Serbian *(Srpski).*

All these languages are similar and mutually understandable, and share the same grammar. The major difference between them is the dialect, with some differences in vocabulary and pronunciation. In some academic and international circles these languages are referred to as BCS or BHS (Bosnian-Croatian / Hrvatski-Serbian) to avoid any unintentional bias. Worldwide today, 21 million people speak a variant of the language formerly named Serbo-Croat.

Serbian uses both the Cyrillic (ћирилица / ćirilica) and the Latin or Roman (latinica /

латиница) scripts. Cyrillic is the official script of Serbia's administration, meaning all government paperwork and written communication should be in Cyrillic, although much is written in both scripts for clarity. All Serbs can write in both scripts, and have two interchangeable writing systems available to them—the choice of script is a matter of personal preference.

The Serbian Cyrillic alphabet was developed by the Serbian linguist Vuk Karadžić in 1814, who created the alphabet on the phonetic principle: "Write as you speak, and read as it is written." The

Latin alphabet system subsequently adopted in Serbia was designed by the Croatian linguist Ljudevit Gaj in 1830, following the same phonetic rules.

While most Serbian words are of Slavic origin, after centuries of influence by neighboring powers a significant number are borrowed from other languages. Through Ottoman influence, the language contains many words of Turkish, Arabic, or Persian origin, especially in southern Serbia and Bosnia. Greek words are used in the Orthodox liturgy, and a few Italian words for foods or greetings are used. Under the influence of the Habsburg monarchy, Serbian adopted many words from Hungarian and

German, as well as French and English. Many of these loanwords are widespread and commonly accepted in the language, especially international words taken from Latin or Greek, and modern technological terms borrowed from English. Hence, with a bit of attention, foreigners can recognize a good many words when written in the Latin alphabet.

The foreign languages most commonly spoken in Serbia are English and German. English is part of the school curriculum from the age of six. German, Russian, and Italian are commonly learned as a second foreign language. Hungarian is widely spoken in the province of Vojvodina.

Serbs are aware that their language can be quite a challenge for foreigners, with its complicated vocabulary, genders, cases, and syntax, and they wouldn't expect to hear a tourist speaking it. Of course, any native would be delighted to hear a foreigner speak a few polite words.

Those wishing to become proficient in Serbian can attend Serbian language courses. The Concord Language School, the Faculty of Philology at Belgrade University, and the Serbian Language and Culture Workshop all offer Serbian language courses mostly in Belgrade.

BODY LANGUAGE

Serbs are open and passionate people: they gesticulate wildly when expressing their feelings or during even the most mundane conversations.

SOME USEFUL PHRASES

	Latin spelling	Cyrillic spelling
Good Day!	*Dobar Dan!*	Добар дан!
I am Tom.	*Ja sam Tom.*	Ја сам Леон.
Pleased to meet you!	*Drago mi je!*	Драго ми је!
How are you?	*Kako ste?*	Како сте?
Good, thank you.	*Dobro hvala.*	Добро хвала.
I live and work in Serbia.	*Zivim i radim u Srbiji.*	Зивим и радим у Србији.
Do you speak English?	*Govorite li engleski?*	Говорите ли енглески?
I'm sorry, I don't understand.	*Izvinite, ne razumem.*	Извините, не разумем.
How much is this?	*Koliko ovo košta?*	Колико ово кошта?
Here you go.	*Izvolite.*	Изволите.
Thank you.	*Hvala.*	Хвала.
Please.	*Molim.*	Молим.
Good bye!	*Dovidjenja!*	Довиђења1
All the best.	*Sve najlepše.*	Све најлепше.

Sharing emotions is part of Serbian culture, so people openly frown when unhappy, or smile when happy.

When talking, Serbs often stand very close to one another and use a great deal of physical contact—they might touch each other's hands, or slap each other on the shoulders. It is not uncommon to see two friends of either sex walking arm in arm, or with their arms over each other's shoulders. Serbs like to kiss, touch, and hug other people in a non-sexual way, and are often oblivious to the fact that a foreign person might feel uncomfortable with the invasion of their personal space.

Serbs don't need much personal space. They stand close to one another in line at the post office or shop, for example. Similarly, they speak loudly, and at such a volume in close proximity as might seem invasive to northern Europeans. However, the volume of a greeting or laughter is considered indicative of the strength of the emotion being communicated, and there is little taste for impassive communication.

Most gestures are common to other countries— nodding the head up and down is "yes," while shaking it from left to right means "no." Shrugging the shoulders means "I don't know," pointing a finger indicates direction or a warning. Holding the first three fingers up, including the thumb, is a nationalist Serbian symbol signifying the unity of the Christian Trinity.

People maintain strong eye contact, and diverting your gaze may be considered rude during a conversation. Eye contact is mandatory when greeting and when clinking glasses. Making eye contact with a stranger on the street and saying a polite *"Dobar dan"* is normal practice.

HUMOR

Serbs love to laugh loudly, and sharing jokes is a big part of social interaction. Even at formal business events, telling a joke can soften the atmosphere or grease the wheels of commerce.

Serbian humor ranges from topics such as food, sex, and sports to religious and political issues. Many jokes are based on punning and wordplay. The aphorism has a long tradition among Serbs, and black humor and satire are also popular. Political satire played an important role during the various social movements, and today is the most popular form of humor across all the media, from newspapers to television to popular music.

As in other parts of the world, many jokes are based on local stereotypes: the people of Vojvodina are seen as phlegmatic and slow; those of southern Serbia are cheapskates; Central Serbs are portrayed as changeable and impulsive; Bosnians are raw and stupid; while Montenegrins are lazy and pushy.

SERBIAN HUMOR

Q: What are the new official Serbian sports disciplines? A: Heavy credit lifting, war hurdles, swimming in debt, running after debtors . . .

Q: What is a democracy? A: I tell you what to do, and you do whatever the hell you want!

The prime minister orders the following budgetary increases: "Allocate an additional two million dinars toward education, six million toward hospitals, and 100 million toward prison improvements." His adviser questions: "With all due respect sir, why so much for prisons?" The prime minister answers: "And where do you think we're going after the next election?"

Q: Why is there no sex between people working in parliament? A: Because they're all related!

SWEARING
Serbs use colorful and juicy language. Swearwords are commonly used in informal situations during everyday exchanges, and without any intention to

insult. This is particularly common among male friends; women are generally considered bad mannered if they use the same language. The words "blood," "mother," "father," "sun," and "god" all feature prominently in the list of top Serbian expletives.

THE MEDIA
Television
Television in Serbia is massively influential and popular. There are currently six broadcast television channels across the country. The public network Radio Television of Serbia broadcasts RTS1 and RTS2, and private networks are Pink, B92, Prva (Fox Serbia), and Happy TV. All channels provide a mix of entertainment, sports, and news content in the Serbian language, or foreign programs with subtitles. Those watching broadcast programming are expected to pay for a TV license.

Vojvodina has a public broadcaster called Radio Television of Vojvodina that airs two channels throughout Vojvodina, RTV1 and RTV2, also available across Serbia via cable. In addition there are almost 150 private regional television channels.

The most convenient way to view digital channels is by cable, provided by a number of different suppliers and offering both Serbian and foreign television stations, mostly from Western Europe. In addition, channels can be received via satellite dish and decoder box, giving access to hundreds of European channels available on the main television satellites such as Astra and Hotbird.

Although plenty of programming is available in English (with Serbian subtitles), news channels are less common. Standard international channels such as CNN, BBC, and Al Jazeera are readily available in most cable and satellite packages.

Radio

Everyone in Serbia listens to the radio. Popular stations can be heard in bars, shops, taxis, coaches, and workplaces, making this one of the most accessible media.

Serbia has around two hundred radio stations with regional or localized coverage, and eight stations with national coverage. Public broadcaster RTS offers the four most popular national stations: RB1, RB2, RB4, and 202; these offer general interest, news, sports, entertainment, music, arts, and business programs in Serbian, and sometimes also in English, French, and Italian. B92 is the country's most popular private radio station, with national coverage and programs in Serbian and English covering news, talk shows, debates, documentaries, interviews, and entertainment. The other stations with national coverage are Radio Index, Focus, and Radio S.

The Press

Serbs are great newspaper readers. Daily papers are sold in newsdealers, kiosks, and stands on most streets. There are currently two daily broadsheets with national coverage, both politically independent:

Politika and *Danas*. There is one middle-market tabloid, *Večernje Novosti*, and four down-market daily tabloids—*Blic*, *Pravda*, *Press*, and *Kurir*. Serbia also has one free (advertiser-funded) newspaper, *24 Sata*, and two daily sports journals with national distribution.

Of the several weekly newspapers and periodicals, the most prominent are *Vreme*, *Nedeljni Telegraf*, and *Nin*, covering local, national, and international news, entertainment, and sports.

Newsdealers also stock a number of weekly magazines covering other subjects such as alternative therapies, medicinal herbalism, cooking, housekeeping, celebrity gossip, light entertainment, children's play, and puzzles.

International magazines such as *The Economist* and *National Geographic*, women's magazines like *Cosmopolitan*, *Elle*, and *Vanity Fair*, and men's magazines such as *Playboy* and *Maxim* can be found in most newsdealers and some bookstores. These will often be local publications, with some unique Serbian content and translated articles.

It is possible to find foreign magazines in French, Italian, and English at some kiosks and bookstores in urban centers. Foreign newspapers are also commonly found in the cities in specialized newsdealers and certain hotels, often a day or two behind the publication date.

SERVICES
Internet and E-mail
Because of the 1990s UN embargo, the Internet was virtually nonexistent in Serbia until the later part of the decade.

Statistics from 2011 indicate that over 50 percent of households in Serbia have Internet connectivity. In rural areas this is often provided by the ISDN dial-up method, while in larger cities broadband access and ADSL are commonly available. Wireless (3G) access is available in every part of Serbia, and wireless dongles and SIM cards can be purchased from most cell phone shops on a pay-as-you-go basis.

Internet access is available in many Internet cafés, with wireless Internet hot spots becoming increasingly popular especially in cafés and hotels across Serbian cities. In smaller towns and remote areas it might be harder to find Internet access in public spaces, so a personal 3G connection is recommended.

Telephones
The international access code for calling Serbia from abroad is +381. The code when dialing out of Serbia is 00, so to call abroad you should dial 00 + country code + local area code + number.

The domestic access code is 0 (not dialed if calling from abroad);

and the local area code is a two- or three-digit code.
Subscriber landline numbers in Serbia total nine to
ten digits including the area code.

Cell phone networks use the domestic access code
0, followed by a two-digit number signifying the
cellular network, always starting with 6, followed by
the six or seven digits of the individual cell number.

Serbia's cell providers offer GSM 900/1800 and 3G
digital technology. If your home country service
provider has a roaming agreement with a carrier in
Serbia, and your phone is compatible, you will be
able to use your cell phone while visiting Serbia.
Otherwise, local SIM cards are easy to find.

Public pay phones can be found across the
country on the streets, in post offices, and in phone
centers. These phones operate by coin or by
prepayment card, or both. Phone cards *(telekart)* can
be purchased at post offices and kiosks. When buying
a phone card you should specify whether you require
an international or local version.

Mailing Services

The postal service in Serbia is a public enterprise
locally known as PTT *(pošta, telegraf i telefon)*, in
existence since the nineteenth century. It is a fairly
good service in terms of cost and reliability. Standard
letters arrive two to five working days after posting;
delays may occur in more remote and mountainous
areas. PTT does not provide postal deliveries on
Saturdays, Sundays, or religious and public holidays.

Post Express, a subdivision of PTT, is the preferred
business postal service, with national deliveries

guaranteed within a twenty-four-hour period. In addition, DHL, UPS, and FedEx all operate in Serbia.

CONCLUSION

Serbia has beautiful landscapes, dynamic cities, and a rich historical legacy. Its geographical diversity offers wonderful opportunities for active outdoor vacations: national parks, rivers, lakes, mountains, canyons, gorges and caves, fertile plains and orchard-covered valleys.

There is something for every taste. Visitors can visit ancient historical sites when cruising the Danube, experience the excitement of skiing in the Kopaonik or Zlatibor Mountains, or relax and rejuvenate in the spa towns of Vrnjačka Banja or Sokobanja. Having connected East with West for centuries, Serbia offers cultural tourists heritage sites and the ruins of empires past. The heart of Serbian spirituality lies in its monasteries and churches, scattered around the country, hidden deep in the mountains, or in locations commanding breathtaking views.

For young backpackers there is one of Europe's biggest music festivals in Novi Sad, set in a medieval fort, and the vibrant nightlife of Belgrade. Business travelers can explore the opportunities of a transition economy and a growing central European market.

Historically, Serbia's strategic position—at the frontiers of the Byzantine and Roman Empires, the Ottoman Empire and the Christian West, and later the Warsaw Pact and NATO—has also brought it wars and devastation. The Serbs still carry the scars of their turbulent past, and tell the stories they have learned about bravery, patriotism, and freedom.

Within one generation the Serbian people have undertaken an epic journey from an authoritarian, monocratic society to an open-minded, democratic one. There are still many demons to overcome, yet Serbia has everything to play for. Even if they sometimes appear abrupt and intrusive, the Serbs are enduring and uncompromising, with a strong sense of warmth and loyalty.

Visitors to Serbia quickly discover the kindness, hospitality, and openness of the people. Without much difficulty, it is possible to meet friendly locals in the street cafés or squares, and with a bit of luck you may be invited to a traditional village to sample real Serbian cooking and home-brewed spirits. Traditional Serbian culture shows the colorful influences of different times and peoples, and the Serbs' passion for these traditions generates a creativity and energy that the foreign visitor cannot fail to appreciate. If you approach Serbians with an open mind, you are bound to find yourself charmed by your company and surroundings!

Further Reading

Andrić, Ivo. *Bosnian Chronicle*. London: Harvill, 1998.

Andrić, Ivo. *Bridge Over The Drina*. London: Harvill, 1994.

Chomsky, Noam. *The New Military Humanism*. London: Pluto, 1999.

Ćirković, Sima M. *The Serbs (The Peoples of Europe)*. Hoboken, NJ: Wiley-Blackwell, 2004.

Ćorović, Vladimir. *Istorija srpskog naroda* (The History of the Serbs). Belgrade: BIGZ, 1989.

Crnjanski, Milos. *Seobe* (Migrations). Belgrade: Novosti, 2004.

Glenny, Misha. *The Balkans 1804–1999: Nationalism, War and the Great Powers*. London: Granta, 2000.

Glenny, Misha. *The Fall of Yugoslavia*. London: Penguin, 1996.

Kiš, Danilo. *A Tomb for Boris Davidovich*. Champaign, IL: Dalkey Archive Press, 2009.

Pantić, Mihajlo. *Novobeogradske price* (New Belgrade Stories). Belgrade: Stubovi kulture, 1998.

Petrović, Goran. *Opsada Crkve Sv. Spasa* (Siege of The Saint Salvation Church). Belgrade: Narodna knjiga/ALFA, 1997.

Stanković, Borisav. *Nečista krv* (Impure Blood). Belgrade: Dereta, 2000.

West, Rebecca. *Black Lamb and Grey Falcon: A Journey Through Yugoslavia*. Edinburgh: Canongate, 2006.

culture smart! serbia

Index